FREE Study Skills DVD Offer

Dear Customer,

Thank you for your purchase from Mometrix! We consider it an honor and a privilege that you have purchased our product and we want to ensure your satisfaction.

As a way of showing our appreciation and to help us better serve you, we have developed a Study Skills DVD that we would like to give you for <u>FREE</u>. This DVD covers our *best practices* for getting ready for your exam, from how to use our study materials to how to best prepare for the day of the test.

All that we ask is that you email us with feedback that would describe your experience so far with our product. Good, bad, or indifferent, we want to know what you think!

To get your FREE Study Skills DVD, email <u>freedvd@mometrix.com</u> with *FREE STUDY SKILLS DVD* in the subject line and the following information in the body of the email:

- The name of the product you purchased.
- Your product rating on a scale of 1-5, with 5 being the highest rating.
- Your feedback. It can be long, short, or anything in between. We just want to know your impressions and experience so far with our product. (Good feedback might include how our study material met your needs and ways we might be able to make it even better. You could highlight features that you found helpful or features that you think we should add.)
- Your full name and shipping address where you would like us to send your free DVD.

If you have any questions or concerns, please don't hesitate to contact me directly.

Thanks again!

Sincerely,

Jay Willis
Vice President
<u>jay.willis@mometrix.com</u>
1-800-673-8175

Property & Casualty Exam SECRETS

Study Guide
Your Key to Exam Success

Mometrix
TEST PREPARATION

Written and edited by the Mometrix Insurance Certification Test Team

Printed in the United States of America

This paper meets the requirements of ANSI/NISO Z39.48-1992 (Permanence of Paper).

Mometrix offers volume discount pricing to institutions. For more information or a price quote, please contact our sales department at sales@mometrix.com or 888-248-1219.

Mometrix Media LLC is not affiliated with or endorsed by any official testing organization. All organizational and test names are trademarks of their respective owners.

Paperback
ISBN 13: 978-1-61072-778-5
ISBN 10: 1-61072-778-9

Ebook
ISBN 13: 978-1-62120-321-6
ISBN 10: 1-62120-321-2

Hardback
ISBN 13: 978-1-5167-0833-8
ISBN 10: 1-5167-0833-4

DEAR FUTURE EXAM SUCCESS STORY

First of all, **THANK YOU** for purchasing Mometrix study materials!

Second, congratulations! You are one of the few determined test-takers who are committed to doing whatever it takes to excel on your exam. **You have come to the right place.** We developed these study materials with one goal in mind: to deliver you the information you need in a format that's concise and easy to use.

In addition to optimizing your guide for the content of the test, we've outlined our recommended steps for breaking down the preparation process into small, attainable goals so you can make sure you stay on track.

We've also analyzed the entire test-taking process, identifying the most common pitfalls and showing how you can overcome them and be ready for any curveball the test throws you.

Standardized testing is one of the biggest obstacles on your road to success, which only increases the importance of doing well in the high-pressure, high-stakes environment of test day. Your results on this test could have a significant impact on your future, and this guide provides the information and practical advice to help you achieve your full potential on test day.

Your success is our success

We would love to hear from you! If you would like to share the story of your exam success or if you have any questions or comments in regard to our products, please contact us at **800-673-8175** or **support@mometrix.com**.

Thanks again for your business and we wish you continued success!

Sincerely,
The Mometrix Test Preparation Team

Need more help? Check out our flashcards at:
http://MometrixFlashcards.com/PropertyCasualty

TABLE OF CONTENTS

Introduction

Thank you for purchasing this resource! You have made the choice to prepare yourself for a test that could have a huge impact on your future, and this guide is designed to help you be fully ready for test day. Obviously, it's important to have a solid understanding of the test material, but you also need to be prepared for the unique environment and stressors of the test, so that you can perform to the best of your abilities.

For this purpose, the first section that appears in this guide is the **Secret Keys**. We've devoted countless hours to meticulously researching what works and what doesn't, and we've boiled down our findings to the five most impactful steps you can take to improve your performance on the test. We start at the beginning with study planning and move through the preparation process, all the way to the testing strategies that will help you get the most out of what you know when you're finally sitting in front of the test.

We recommend that you start preparing for your test as far in advance as possible. However, if you've bought this guide as a last-minute study resource and only have a few days before your test, we recommend that you skip over the first two Secret Keys since they address a long-term study plan.

If you struggle with **test anxiety**, we strongly encourage you to check out our recommendations for how you can overcome it. Test anxiety is a formidable foe, but it can be beaten, and we want to make sure you have the tools you need to defeat it.

Secret Key #1 – Plan Big, Study Small

There's a lot riding on your performance. If you want to ace this test, you're going to need to keep your skills sharp and the material fresh in your mind. You need a plan that lets you review everything you need to know while still fitting in your schedule. We'll break this strategy down into three categories.

Information Organization

Start with the information you already have: the official test outline. From this, you can make a complete list of all the concepts you need to cover before the test. Organize these concepts into groups that can be studied together, and create a list of any related vocabulary you need to learn so you can brush up on any difficult terms. You'll want to keep this vocabulary list handy once you actually start studying since you may need to add to it along the way.

Time Management

Once you have your set of study concepts, decide how to spread them out over the time you have left before the test. Break your study plan into small, clear goals so you have a manageable task for each day and know exactly what you're doing. Then just focus on one small step at a time. When you manage your time this way, you don't need to spend hours at a time studying. Studying a small block of content for a short period each day helps you retain information better and avoid stressing over how much you have left to do. You can relax knowing that you have a plan to cover everything in time. In order for this strategy to be effective though, you have to start studying early and stick to your schedule. Avoid the exhaustion and futility that comes from last-minute cramming!

Study Environment

The environment you study in has a big impact on your learning. Studying in a coffee shop, while probably more enjoyable, is not likely to be as fruitful as studying in a quiet room. It's important to keep distractions to a minimum. You're only planning to study for a short block of time, so make the most of it. Don't pause to check your phone or get up to find a snack. It's also important to **avoid multitasking**. Research has consistently shown that multitasking will make your studying dramatically less effective. Your study area should also be comfortable and well-lit so you don't have the distraction of straining your eyes or sitting on an uncomfortable chair.

The time of day you study is also important. You want to be rested and alert. Don't wait until just before bedtime. Study when you'll be most likely to comprehend and remember. Even better, if you know what time of day your test will be, set that time aside for study. That way your brain will be used to working on that subject at that specific time and you'll have a better chance of recalling information.

Finally, it can be helpful to team up with others who are studying for the same test. Your actual studying should be done in as isolated an environment as possible, but the work of organizing the information and setting up the study plan can be divided up. In between study sessions, you can discuss with your teammates the concepts that you're all studying and quiz each other on the details. Just be sure that your teammates are as serious about the test as you are. If you find that your study time is being replaced with social time, you might need to find a new team.

Secret Key #2 – Make Your Studying Count

You're devoting a lot of time and effort to preparing for this test, so you want to be absolutely certain it will pay off. This means doing more than just reading the content and hoping you can remember it on test day. It's important to make every minute of study count. There are two main areas you can focus on to make your studying count:

Retention

It doesn't matter how much time you study if you can't remember the material. You need to make sure you are retaining the concepts. To check your retention of the information you're learning, try recalling it at later times with minimal prompting. Try carrying around flashcards and glance at one or two from time to time or ask a friend who's also studying for the test to quiz you.

To enhance your retention, look for ways to put the information into practice so that you can apply it rather than simply recalling it. If you're using the information in practical ways, it will be much easier to remember. Similarly, it helps to solidify a concept in your mind if you're not only reading it to yourself but also explaining it to someone else. Ask a friend to let you teach them about a concept you're a little shaky on (or speak aloud to an imaginary audience if necessary). As you try to summarize, define, give examples, and answer your friend's questions, you'll understand the concepts better and they will stay with you longer. Finally, step back for a big picture view and ask yourself how each piece of information fits with the whole subject. When you link the different concepts together and see them working together as a whole, it's easier to remember the individual components.

Finally, practice showing your work on any multi-step problems, even if you're just studying. Writing out each step you take to solve a problem will help solidify the process in your mind, and you'll be more likely to remember it during the test.

Modality

Modality simply refers to the means or method by which you study. Choosing a study modality that fits your own individual learning style is crucial. No two people learn best in exactly the same way, so it's important to know your strengths and use them to your advantage.

For example, if you learn best by visualization, focus on visualizing a concept in your mind and draw an image or a diagram. Try color-coding your notes, illustrating them, or creating symbols that will trigger your mind to recall a learned concept. If you learn best by hearing or discussing information, find a study partner who learns the same way or read aloud to yourself. Think about how to put the information in your own words. Imagine that you are giving a lecture on the topic and record yourself so you can listen to it later.

For any learning style, flashcards can be helpful. Organize the information so you can take advantage of spare moments to review. Underline key words or phrases. Use different colors for different categories. Mnemonic devices (such as creating a short list in which every item starts with the same letter) can also help with retention. Find what works best for you and use it to store the information in your mind most effectively and easily.

Secret Key #3 – Practice the Right Way

Your success on test day depends not only on how many hours you put into preparing, but also on whether you prepared the right way. It's good to check along the way to see if your studying is paying off. One of the most effective ways to do this is by taking practice tests to evaluate your progress. Practice tests are useful because they show exactly where you need to improve. Every time you take a practice test, pay special attention to these three groups of questions:

- The questions you got wrong
- The questions you had to guess on, even if you guessed right
- The questions you found difficult or slow to work through

This will show you exactly what your weak areas are, and where you need to devote more study time. Ask yourself why each of these questions gave you trouble. Was it because you didn't understand the material? Was it because you didn't remember the vocabulary? Do you need more repetitions on this type of question to build speed and confidence? Dig into those questions and figure out how you can strengthen your weak areas as you go back to review the material.

Additionally, many practice tests have a section explaining the answer choices. It can be tempting to read the explanation and think that you now have a good understanding of the concept. However, an explanation likely only covers part of the question's broader context. Even if the explanation makes sense, **go back and investigate** every concept related to the question until you're positive you have a thorough understanding.

As you go along, keep in mind that the practice test is just that: practice. Memorizing these questions and answers will not be very helpful on the actual test because it is unlikely to have any of the same exact questions. If you only know the right answers to the sample questions, you won't be prepared for the real thing. **Study the concepts** until you understand them fully, and then you'll be able to answer any question that shows up on the test.

It's important to wait on the practice tests until you're ready. If you take a test on your first day of study, you may be overwhelmed by the amount of material covered and how much you need to learn. Work up to it gradually.

On test day, you'll need to be prepared for answering questions, managing your time, and using the test-taking strategies you've learned. It's a lot to balance, like a mental marathon that will have a big impact on your future. Like training for a marathon, you'll need to start slowly and work your way up. When test day arrives, you'll be ready.

Start with the strategies you've read in the first two Secret Keys—plan your course and study in the way that works best for you. If you have time, consider using multiple study resources to get different approaches to the same concepts. It can be helpful to see difficult concepts from more than one angle. Then find a good source for practice tests. Many times, the test website will suggest potential study resources or provide sample tests.

Practice Test Strategy

If you're able to find at least three practice tests, we recommend this strategy:

UNTIMED AND OPEN-BOOK PRACTICE

Take the first test with no time constraints and with your notes and study guide handy. Take your time and focus on applying the strategies you've learned.

TIMED AND OPEN-BOOK PRACTICE

Take the second practice test open-book as well, but set a timer and practice pacing yourself to finish in time.

TIMED AND CLOSED-BOOK PRACTICE

Take any other practice tests as if it were test day. Set a timer and put away your study materials. Sit at a table or desk in a quiet room, imagine yourself at the testing center, and answer questions as quickly and accurately as possible.

Keep repeating timed and closed-book tests on a regular basis until you run out of practice tests or it's time for the actual test. Your mind will be ready for the schedule and stress of test day, and you'll be able to focus on recalling the material you've learned.

Secret Key #4 – Pace Yourself

Once you're fully prepared for the material on the test, your biggest challenge on test day will be managing your time. Just knowing that the clock is ticking can make you panic even if you have plenty of time left. Work on pacing yourself so you can build confidence against the time constraints of the exam. Pacing is a difficult skill to master, especially in a high-pressure environment, so **practice is vital**.

Set time expectations for your pace based on how much time is available. For example, if a section has 60 questions and the time limit is 30 minutes, you know you have to average 30 seconds or less per question in order to answer them all. Although 30 seconds is the hard limit, set 25 seconds per question as your goal, so you reserve extra time to spend on harder questions. When you budget extra time for the harder questions, you no longer have any reason to stress when those questions take longer to answer.

Don't let this time expectation distract you from working through the test at a calm, steady pace, but keep it in mind so you don't spend too much time on any one question. Recognize that taking extra time on one question you don't understand may keep you from answering two that you do understand later in the test. If your time limit for a question is up and you're still not sure of the answer, mark it and move on, and come back to it later if the time and the test format allow. If the testing format doesn't allow you to return to earlier questions, just make an educated guess; then put it out of your mind and move on.

On the easier questions, be careful not to rush. It may seem wise to hurry through them so you have more time for the challenging ones, but it's not worth missing one if you know the concept and just didn't take the time to read the question fully. Work efficiently but make sure you understand the question and have looked at all of the answer choices, since more than one may seem right at first.

Even if you're paying attention to the time, you may find yourself a little behind at some point. You should speed up to get back on track, but do so wisely. Don't panic; just take a few seconds less on each question until you're caught up. Don't guess without thinking, but do look through the answer choices and eliminate any you know are wrong. If you can get down to two choices, it is often worthwhile to guess from those. Once you've chosen an answer, move on and don't dwell on any that you skipped or had to hurry through. If a question was taking too long, chances are it was one of the harder ones, so you weren't as likely to get it right anyway.

On the other hand, if you find yourself getting ahead of schedule, it may be beneficial to slow down a little. The more quickly you work, the more likely you are to make a careless mistake that will affect your score. You've budgeted time for each question, so don't be afraid to spend that time. Practice an efficient but careful pace to get the most out of the time you have.

Secret Key #5 – Have a Plan for Guessing

When you're taking the test, you may find yourself stuck on a question. Some of the answer choices seem better than others, but you don't see the one answer choice that is obviously correct. What do you do?

The scenario described above is very common, yet most test takers have not effectively prepared for it. Developing and practicing a plan for guessing may be one of the single most effective uses of your time as you get ready for the exam.

In developing your plan for guessing, there are three questions to address:

- When should you start the guessing process?
- How should you narrow down the choices?
- Which answer should you choose?

When to Start the Guessing Process

Unless your plan for guessing is to select C every time (which, despite its merits, is not what we recommend), you need to leave yourself enough time to apply your answer elimination strategies. Since you have a limited amount of time for each question, that means that if you're going to give yourself the best shot at guessing correctly, you have to decide quickly whether or not you will guess.

Of course, the best-case scenario is that you don't have to guess at all, so first, see if you can answer the question based on your knowledge of the subject and basic reasoning skills. Focus on the key words in the question and try to jog your memory of related topics. Give yourself a chance to bring the knowledge to mind, but once you realize that you don't have (or you can't access) the knowledge you need to answer the question, it's time to start the guessing process.

It's almost always better to start the guessing process too early than too late. It only takes a few seconds to remember something and answer the question from knowledge. Carefully eliminating wrong answer choices takes longer. Plus, going through the process of eliminating answer choices can actually help jog your memory.

Summary: Start the guessing process as soon as you decide that you can't answer the question based on your knowledge.

How to Narrow Down the Choices

The next chapter in this book (**Test-Taking Strategies**) includes a wide range of strategies for how to approach questions and how to look for answer choices to eliminate. You will definitely want to read those carefully, practice them, and figure out which ones work best for you. Here though, we're going to address a mindset rather than a particular strategy.

Your chances of guessing an answer correctly depend on how many options you are choosing from.

How many choices you have	How likely you are to guess correctly
5	20%
4	25%
3	33%
2	50%
1	100%

You can see from this chart just how valuable it is to be able to eliminate incorrect answers and make an educated guess, but there are two things that many test takers do that cause them to miss out on the benefits of guessing:

- Accidentally eliminating the correct answer
- Selecting an answer based on an impression

We'll look at the first one here, and the second one in the next section.

To avoid accidentally eliminating the correct answer, we recommend a thought exercise called **the $5 challenge**. In this challenge, you only eliminate an answer choice from contention if you are willing to bet $5 on it being wrong. Why $5? Five dollars is a small but not insignificant amount of money. It's an amount you could afford to lose but wouldn't want to throw away. And while losing $5 once might not hurt too much, doing it twenty times will set you back $100. In the same way, each small decision you make—eliminating a choice here, guessing on a question there—won't by itself impact your score very much, but when you put them all together, they can make a big difference. By holding each answer choice elimination decision to a higher standard, you can reduce the risk of accidentally eliminating the correct answer.

The $5 challenge can also be applied in a positive sense: If you are willing to bet $5 that an answer choice *is* correct, go ahead and mark it as correct.

Summary: Only eliminate an answer choice if you are willing to bet $5 that it is wrong.

8

Which Answer to Choose

You're taking the test. You've run into a hard question and decided you'll have to guess. You've eliminated all the answer choices you're willing to bet $5 on. Now you have to pick an answer. Why do we even need to talk about this? Why can't you just pick whichever one you feel like when the time comes?

The answer to these questions is that if you don't come into the test with a plan, you'll rely on your impression to select an answer choice, and if you do that, you risk falling into a trap. The test writers know that everyone who takes their test will be guessing on some of the questions, so they intentionally write wrong answer choices to seem plausible. You still have to pick an answer though, and if the wrong answer choices are designed to look right, how can you ever be sure that you're not falling for their trap? The best solution we've found to this dilemma is to take the decision out of your hands entirely. Here is the process we recommend:

Once you've eliminated any choices that you are confident (willing to bet $5) are wrong, select the first remaining choice as your answer.

Whether you choose to select the first remaining choice, the second, or the last, the important thing is that you use some preselected standard. Using this approach guarantees that you will not be enticed into selecting an answer choice that looks right, because you are not basing your decision on how the answer choices look.

This is not meant to make you question your knowledge. Instead, it is to help you recognize the difference between your knowledge and your impressions. There's a huge difference between thinking an answer is right because of what you know, and thinking an answer is right because it looks or sounds like it should be right.

Summary: To ensure that your selection is appropriately random, make a predetermined selection from among all answer choices you have not eliminated.

Test-Taking Strategies

This section contains a list of test-taking strategies that you may find helpful as you work through the test. By taking what you know and applying logical thought, you can maximize your chances of answering any question correctly!

It is very important to realize that every question is different and every person is different: no single strategy will work on every question, and no single strategy will work for every person. That's why we've included all of them here, so you can try them out and determine which ones work best for different types of questions and which ones work best for you.

Question Strategies

READ CAREFULLY

Read the question and answer choices carefully. Don't miss the question because you misread the terms. You have plenty of time to read each question thoroughly and make sure you understand what is being asked. Yet a happy medium must be attained, so don't waste too much time. You must read carefully, but efficiently.

CONTEXTUAL CLUES

Look for contextual clues. If the question includes a word you are not familiar with, look at the immediate context for some indication of what the word might mean. Contextual clues can often give you all the information you need to decipher the meaning of an unfamiliar word. Even if you can't determine the meaning, you may be able to narrow down the possibilities enough to make a solid guess at the answer to the question.

PREFIXES

If you're having trouble with a word in the question or answer choices, try dissecting it. Take advantage of every clue that the word might include. Prefixes and suffixes can be a huge help. Usually they allow you to determine a basic meaning. Pre- means before, post- means after, pro - is positive, de- is negative. From prefixes and suffixes, you can get an idea of the general meaning of the word and try to put it into context.

HEDGE WORDS

Watch out for critical hedge words, such as *likely, may, can, sometimes, often, almost, mostly, usually, generally, rarely,* and *sometimes.* Question writers insert these hedge phrases to cover every possibility. Often an answer choice will be wrong simply because it leaves no room for exception. Be on guard for answer choices that have definitive words such as *exactly* and *always.*

SWITCHBACK WORDS

Stay alert for *switchbacks.* These are the words and phrases frequently used to alert you to shifts in thought. The most common switchback words are *but, although,* and *however.* Others include *nevertheless, on the other hand, even though, while, in spite of, despite, regardless of.* Switchback words are important to catch because they can change the direction of the question or an answer choice.

FACE VALUE

When in doubt, use common sense. Accept the situation in the problem at face value. Don't read too much into it. These problems will not require you to make wild assumptions. If you have to go beyond creativity and warp time or space in order to have an answer choice fit the question, then you should move on and consider the other answer choices. These are normal problems rooted in reality. The applicable relationship or explanation may not be readily apparent, but it is there for you to figure out. Use your common sense to interpret anything that isn't clear.

Answer Choice Strategies

ANSWER SELECTION

The most thorough way to pick an answer choice is to identify and eliminate wrong answers until only one is left, then confirm it is the correct answer. Sometimes an answer choice may immediately seem right, but be careful. The test writers will usually put more than one reasonable answer choice on each question, so take a second to read all of them and make sure that the other choices are not equally obvious. As long as you have time left, it is better to read every answer choice than to pick the first one that looks right without checking the others.

ANSWER CHOICE FAMILIES

An answer choice family consists of two (in rare cases, three) answer choices that are very similar in construction and cannot all be true at the same time. If you see two answer choices that are direct opposites or parallels, one of them is usually the correct answer. For instance, if one answer choice says that quantity x increases and another either says that quantity x decreases (opposite) or says that quantity y increases (parallel), then those answer choices would fall into the same family. An answer choice that doesn't match the construction of the answer choice family is more likely to be incorrect. Most questions will not have answer choice families, but when they do appear, you should be prepared to recognize them.

ELIMINATE ANSWERS

Eliminate answer choices as soon as you realize they are wrong, but make sure you consider all possibilities. If you are eliminating answer choices and realize that the last one you are left with is also wrong, don't panic. Start over and consider each choice again. There may be something you missed the first time that you will realize on the second pass.

AVOID FACT TRAPS

Don't be distracted by an answer choice that is factually true but doesn't answer the question. You are looking for the choice that answers the question. Stay focused on what the question is asking for so you don't accidentally pick an answer that is true but incorrect. Always go back to the question and make sure the answer choice you've selected actually answers the question and is not merely a true statement.

EXTREME STATEMENTS

In general, you should avoid answers that put forth extreme actions as standard practice or proclaim controversial ideas as established fact. An answer choice that states the "process should be used in certain situations, if..." is much more likely to be correct than one that states the "process should be discontinued completely." The first is a calm rational statement and doesn't even make a definitive, uncompromising stance, using a hedge word *if* to provide wiggle room, whereas the second choice is a radical idea and far more extreme.

BENCHMARK

As you read through the answer choices and you come across one that seems to answer the question well, mentally select that answer choice. This is not your final answer, but it's the one that will help you evaluate the other answer choices. The one that you selected is your benchmark or standard for judging each of the other answer choices. Every other answer choice must be compared to your benchmark. That choice is correct until proven otherwise by another answer choice beating it. If you find a better answer, then that one becomes your new benchmark. Once you've decided that no other choice answers the question as well as your benchmark, you have your final answer.

PREDICT THE ANSWER

Before you even start looking at the answer choices, it is often best to try to predict the answer. When you come up with the answer on your own, it is easier to avoid distractions and traps because you will know exactly what to look for. The right answer choice is unlikely to be word-for-word what you came up with, but it should be a close match. Even if you are confident that you have the right answer, you should still take the time to read each option before moving on.

General Strategies

TOUGH QUESTIONS

If you are stumped on a problem or it appears too hard or too difficult, don't waste time. Move on! Remember though, if you can quickly check for obviously incorrect answer choices, your chances of guessing correctly are greatly improved. Before you completely give up, at least try to knock out a couple of possible answers. Eliminate what you can and then guess at the remaining answer choices before moving on.

CHECK YOUR WORK

Since you will probably not know every term listed and the answer to every question, it is important that you get credit for the ones that you do know. Don't miss any questions through careless mistakes. If at all possible, try to take a second to look back over your answer selection and make sure you've selected the correct answer choice and haven't made a costly careless mistake (such as marking an answer choice that you didn't mean to mark). This quick double check should more than pay for itself in caught mistakes for the time it costs.

PACE YOURSELF

It's easy to be overwhelmed when you're looking at a page full of questions; your mind is confused and full of random thoughts, and the clock is ticking down faster than you would like. Calm down and maintain the pace that you have set for yourself. Especially as you get down to the last few minutes of the test, don't let the small numbers on the clock make you panic. As long as you are on track by monitoring your pace, you are guaranteed to have time for each question.

DON'T RUSH

It is very easy to make errors when you are in a hurry. Maintaining a fast pace in answering questions is pointless if it makes you miss questions that you would have gotten right otherwise. Test writers like to include distracting information and wrong answers that seem right. Taking a little extra time to avoid careless mistakes can make all the difference in your test score. Find a pace that allows you to be confident in the answers that you select.

KEEP MOVING

Panicking will not help you pass the test, so do your best to stay calm and keep moving. Taking deep breaths and going through the answer elimination steps you practiced can help to break through a stress barrier and keep your pace.

Final Notes

The combination of a solid foundation of content knowledge and the confidence that comes from practicing your plan for applying that knowledge is the key to maximizing your performance on test day. As your foundation of content knowledge is built up and strengthened, you'll find that the strategies included in this chapter become more and more effective in helping you quickly sift through the distractions and traps of the test to isolate the correct answer.

Now it's time to move on to the test content chapters of this book, but be sure to keep your goal in mind. As you read, think about how you will be able to apply this information on the test. If you've already seen sample questions for the test and you have an idea of the question format and style, try to come up with questions of your own that you can answer based on what you're reading. This will give you valuable practice applying your knowledge in the same ways you can expect to on test day.

Good luck and good studying!

Types of Property Policies

HOMEOWNER'S INSURANCE

Homeowner's insurance is a personal, multi-line (property and casualty) policy with the following eligibility requirements:

- Only the owner/occupant of a dwelling and renters with residential occupancies are eligible for coverage.
- The dwelling must consist of four or fewer family units, and each family can have a maximum of two roomers or boarders.
- A dwelling is only eligible if it is exclusively a residence. However, allowances can be made for **incidental occupancies** (including private schools, studios, offices, etc.).
- The following dwellings are eligible: dwellings under construction, seasonal/secondary residences, homes being paid off under installment contracts, homes occupied under life estates and trustees, and mobile homes (as long as the Mobile Home endorsement has been purchased).
- Farms are not eligible.
- The insured must purchase both lines (property and casualty) unless he is renting the property.

Homeowner's insurance policies are divided into a **property insurance section** (section I) and a **liability and medical insurance section** (section II). Every type of policy provides the same liability coverage. Policies differ only in the level of property coverage they offer.

HO-2, also known as **the broad form**, protects against named perils, such as theft and glass breakage. It also offers the option to extend coverage to vandalism and malicious mischief. HO-2 forms cover personal property and dwellings, and are intended for owner/occupants of one, two, three, or four family homes.

HO-3, also known as **the special form**, extends open peril protection to the dwelling and other structures, and named peril protection for unscheduled personal property under Coverage C. The open peril protection also covers loss of use of real property (the dwelling and other structures).

HO-4, also known as **the contents broad form**, **the tenant's form**, or **the renter's form**, provides named peril protection for the personal property of tenants—those who rent (but do not own) apartments, mobile homes, condominiums, and single-family homes. HO-4 provides the same protection as HO-2, but only covers personal property, not dwellings. It also provides limited insurance coverage for improvements and additions if the owner has paid for their installation.

HO-5, also known as **the comprehensive owner's form**, extends open peril protection to personal property. It also protects the dwelling and other structures, and covers loss of use. This policy is intended for individuals who own and occupy one, two, three, and four family homes.

HO-6, also known as **the condominium unit owner's form**, extends named peril protection to the personal property of condominium or cooperative owners. HO-6 provides a level of personal property insurance that is very similar to HO-2, HO-3, and HO-4. Loss assessments are covered up to a limit of $1,000.

HO-8, also known as the **modified coverage form for special risks**, is intended for uniquely constructed properties and older properties whose replacement costs are substantially higher than

15

their market values. This form extends basic named peril protection to dwellings and personal property, and offers extended coverage for certain perils, as well as vandalism and malicious mischief. Loss settlements are paid on an actual cash value basis.

COVERAGES A, B, C, AND D

Coverage A—dwelling insures the dwelling and any attached structures. It also covers any fixtures or materials used to maintain the dwelling, as long as they are attached to or located on the premises. On HO-6 forms, Coverage A has a standard limit of $1,000 per occurrence.

Coverage B—other structures insures other buildings that are located on the same premises, but are separate from the dwelling (though they may be connected by a utility line or fence). The maximum coverage amount is 10% of Coverage A's limit. Coverage B does not cover structures used for business-related purposes, nor does it cover properties rented to persons, unless the person is a tenant of the dwelling. It does, however, cover private garages.

Coverage C—personal property covers the insured's personal property, regardless of where in the world it is located. If the insured so desires, Coverage C can also cover:

- The personal property of the insured's guests and employees in any residence the insured occupies.
- The personal property of others if their property and the insured's are located in the same area of the insured's residence.

Coverage C provides global personal property coverage for a limited time period. Consequently, for personal property that is stored away from the insured's residence, coverage is limited to $1,000 or 10% of Coverage C's limit, whichever is greater. If the insured is moving to a new principle residence, his personal property is fully covered for a maximum of 30 days. If the insured's residence is being repaired or has been declared uninhabitable, his personal property is fully covered while it is at a temporary residence.

On homeowner's insurance policies, Coverage C imposes **special liability limits**, also known as **sublimits**, which provide less coverage than the policy limit for certain categories of property. These sublimits include the following:

- $200 on money, coins, precious metals, and similar property
- $1,500 on securities, deeds, passports, manuscripts, and other pieces of paper property
- $500 on business-related property kept off the residential premises
- $2,500 on business-related property kept on the residential premises
- $1,500 on electronic accessories that are powered by both a car and a motor vehicle while they are in or separated from the vehicle
- $1,500 on business-related electronic accessories that are not part of a motor vehicle
- $1,500 on watercraft and all related trailers and equipment
- $1,500 on trailers not associated with watercraft
- $1,500 on theft of jewelry, precious stones, watches, and furs
- $2,500 on theft of firearms
- $2,500 on silverware, pewterware, and goldware

On homeowner's insurance policies, Coverage C does not cover the following classes of property:

- Roomers' property
- Rental property that is part of an apartment

- Animals, fish, and birds
- Motorized vehicles, aircraft, hovercraft, and their equipment and parts
- Business information records (both electronic and paper-based), unless the records are pre-recorded programs that are sold commercially
- Water/steam
- Credit cards
- Rental property held by others if it is located somewhere other than the residence

Coverage D—loss of use reimburses the insured if a dwelling is rendered uninhabitable by a covered loss. There are two possible methods of reimbursement:

1. **Additional living expense** – If the dwelling is the insured's residence, the policy allows the insured to preserve his typical standard of living.
2. **Fair rental value** – If the insured is renting out the dwelling to another person, the policy repays any lost rent payments.

Additional coverages are automatically included on policy forms in addendum to the policy's major coverages.

General debris removal reimburses the cost of removing debris if the damage was caused by a covered peril. This coverage does not extend to trees. Most policies increase the maximum available coverage by 5% when the combined cost of property damage and debris removal is greater than the policy limit.

Tree debris removal covers the following expenses:

- Removing the insured's tree if it is knocked down by wind, hail, or weight of ice, sleet, or snow
- Removing a neighbor's tree if it is knocked down by any peril included under Coverage C

This coverage is not applicable unless one of the following conditions is present: the tree has damaged a covered structure; the tree is blocking the entrance to a driveway; the tree is blocking a handicap accessible feature. Coverage is limited to $1,000 per occurrence and $500 per tree.

Trees, shrubs, and other plants insures trees, shrubs, and other plants if they are damaged or lost due to fire, explosion, lightning, riot, theft, V&MM, and aircraft (provided it is not owned or operated by an insured). On most policies, coverage cannot exceed 5% of Coverage A's limit, or $500 per tree, shrub, or plant. On HO-4 and HO-6 policies, coverage cannot exceed 10% of Coverage C's limit, or $500 per tree, shrub, or plant.

Reasonable repairs reimburses the insured for any reasonable costs that he must pay in order to repair damage caused by a covered peril. These repairs must be necessary to protect the property against additional damage and loss.

Property removed insures property as it is being moved from a location that is threatened by a covered peril. This coverage lasts a maximum of 30 days.

Loss assessment reimburses a maximum of $1,000 for loss assessments required by a corporation or property owners' association. The loss assessment must be necessitated by a covered peril that causes a direct loss to property owned collectively by all members in the association. Consider, for example, a stairwell in a condominium building. The stairwell is considered community property, or property owned collectively by each condominium owner in the building. Assume the stairwell

17

is damaged by a covered peril, forcing the condominium owners' association to conduct a loss assessment. Each owner in the building is required to pay a portion of the assessment. If an owner has homeowner's insurance, the loss assessment coverage would pay his part of the assessment.

Fire department service charge provides a maximum of $500 to pay the fire department when it must save or protect covered property. This additional coverage does not include a deductible, and cannot be obtained inside city limits where fire department services are provided.

Credit card, electronic fund transfer card or access device, forgery, and counterfeit money provides a maximum of $500 when the insured is legally obligated to pay losses caused by the following:

- Stealing or illegally using the insured's cards
- Accepting counterfeit money in good faith
- Forging or altering the insured's checks

This coverage does not include a deductible, and does not cover losses caused by the insured's own business operations or dishonesty.

Collapse insures property against physical loss resulting from building collapse, as long as it is caused by a covered or additional peril. This coverage is available on HO-2, HO-3, HO-4, HO-5, and HO-6.

Landlord's furnishings insures appliances, carpeting, and various household items within apartments that are located on residence premises and are being rented or held for rental by the insured. This coverage provides a maximum limit of $2,500, and is only available on HO-2, HO-3, and HO-5.

Grave markers insure grave markers and mausoleums against perils included under Coverage C. The coverage limit is $5,000, and is available on HO-2, HO-3, HO-4, HO-5, and HO-6.

Glass or safety glazing material insures against glass breakage in a building, and covers property like windows and storm doors.

Building additions and alterations insures installations, fixtures, and improvements if the insured has paid for their construction. This coverage has a maximum limit of 10% of Coverage C's amount, and is only available for HO-4.

Ordinance or law coverage provides a maximum of 10% of Coverage A's limit when the insured must rebuild or repair structures to conform to new building laws or land use codes. This coverage is available on HO-2, HO-3, HO-4, HO-5, and HO-6.

BASIC PERILS

All homeowner's insurance policies cover the following basic perils:

- Windstorm and hail – Interior damage is only covered if the wind or hail makes a hole in the building before the damage occurs. Watercraft and similar equipment are only protected if they are stored inside a fully enclosed building.
- Fire/Explosion
- Lightning
- Smoke – This includes puffback, which encompasses emissions from furnaces and boilers (but not fireplaces), agricultural smudging, or industrial functions.

- Vandalism and malicious mischief, also known as V&MM (unless the structure has bee vacant for 60 or more consecutive days)
- Vehicles (unless they are owned or operated by the insured or residents of the insured property)
- Aircraft
- Riot and civil unrest
- Volcanic eruption
- Theft (except in the following situations: theft committed by the insured; theft involving a dwelling under construction, a rental part of the premises, or watercraft and related equipment; mysterious disappearances)

PERILS COVERED ON BROAD FORM (HO-2)

The broad form, or HO-2, covers all the basic perils, as well as the following expanded perils:

- Weight of ice, sleet, or snow, unless it damages fences, patios, awnings, pavement, swimming pools, piers, bulkheads, docks, or similar structures
- Falling objects (which must first damage an exterior surface)
- Freezing of water systems, such as plumbing (If the dwelling is unoccupied, this coverage only applies if the insured has taken the necessary precautions to avoid freezing.)
- Sudden and accidental overflow from water/steam systems (On HO-6 forms, this coverage also includes the cost of removing and replacing damaged systems.)
- Accidental breakage of water/steam systems
- Sudden and accidental discharge of artificial electric current (except damage to electrical components such as transistors)
- Vehicle damage to fences, driveways, and walkways (even if the vehicle is owned or operated by a resident of the insured property)
- Smoke damage from fireplaces

These coverages are included on HO-2, HO-4, and HO-6 forms.

EXCLUSIONS INCLUDED ON SPECIAL FORM (HO-3)

The special form, or HO-3, is an open peril policy. It covers any risk of direct physical loss to the dwelling (Coverage A) and other structures (Coverage B) except for the following losses, which are specifically excluded by the policy:

- Collapse, unless it is included under other coverages section
- Theft involving a building under construction
- Vandalism and malicious mischief (V&MM) involving a building that has been vacant for longer than 60 consecutive days
- Freezing of plumbing, heating, and similar systems when the building is under construction, unoccupied, or vacant, unless the insured took the necessary precautions
- Water or ice damage (freezing, thawing, weight, and pressure) to fences, patios, pavements, foundations, swimming pools, retaining walls, bulkheads, docks, and similar structures
- Damage from animals and insects if they are owned by the insured
- Cracking, shrinking, expanding, and bulging of pavements, foundations, walls, and similar surfaces
- Natural wear and tear, rust, corrosion, agricultural smudging, and other gradual, expected losses
- Emission of smoke, vapor, chemicals, fumes, waste, and similar pollutants

19

PERILS COVERED ON COMPREHENSIVE FORM (HO-5)

The comprehensive form, or HO-5, provides open peril protection for dwellings, other structures, and personal property. It has the same exclusions found on Coverages A and B of the special form (HO-3). There are, however, a few differences. With respect to theft coverage, HO-5 forms also insure personal property that has been lost, misplaced, or subject to mysterious disappearance. Glassware, eyeglasses, bric-a-brac, porcelain, statues, and other highly fragile personal articles receive limited coverage. HO-5 insures against the following perils:

- Fire
- Lightning
- Vandalism and malicious mischief (V&MM)
- Theft
- Building collapse
- Certain types of water damage
- Sudden and accidental damage from a water heating, air conditioning, or sprinkler system
- Extended coverage perils

EXCLUSIONS AND CONDITIONS FOUND ON ALL HOMEOWNER'S INSURANCE POLICIES

Homeowner's policies generally exclude coverage for losses resulting from the following:

- Earthquake and similar kinds of earth movement
- Flooding and water overflow
- War
- Nuclear risk
- Building addition, repair, or demolition due to new laws or ordinances
- Power outages if the source is located off the premises
- Government seizure or demolition of property
- Intentional action on the insured's behalf
- Damage caused by the insured's failure to take appropriate action after a loss

Standard conditions on homeowner's policies include the following: **duties after a loss**, **pair or set**, **mortgage**, **other insurance**, **appraisal**, and **loss settlement**. According to the loss settlement condition, if the insured meets an 80% coinsurance condition, he or she is reimbursed the replacement cost for losses to the dwelling and other structures. For personal property, non-building structures, and carpeting, awnings, outdoor antennas, outdoor equipment, and appliances, the settlement is made by reimbursing the actual cash value. This cannot exceed the repair or replacement cost.

CALCULATING POLICY LIMITS

The following chart explains how policy limits are determined for each type of homeowner's insurance:

Determining Policy Limits for HO-2, HO-3, HO-5, and HO-8	Determining Policy Limits for HO-4 and HO-6
Coverage A policy limit = primary limit determined by insured	Coverage A policy limit = N/A
Coverage B policy limit = 10% of Coverage A's limit for 1 to 2 family dwellings, or 5% of Coverage A's limit for 3 to 4 family dwellings	Coverage B policy limit = N/A

Coverage C policy limit = 50% of Coverage A's limit for 1 to 2 family dwellings, 30% of Coverage A's limit for 3 family dwellings, or 25% of Coverage A's limit for four family dwellings	Coverage C policy limit = primary limit determined by insured
Coverage D policy limit = 10% of Coverage A's limit for HO-8, or 30% of Coverage A's limit for HO-2, HO-3, or HO-5	Coverage D policy limit = 50% of Coverage C's limit for HO-6, or 30% of Coverage C's limit for HO-4

The above limits represent the minimum amounts of available coverage; higher coverage may be available.

COVERAGES E AND F

Coverage E—Personal Liability is a type of liability coverage available on all homeowner's policies. It covers the insured when he is found liable for another person's **bodily injury** or **property damage**. The policy limit for Coverage E is $100,000 in damages per occurrence. In addition to this limit, the insurer agrees to pay court costs and prejudgment interest. However, the insurer will not cover any additional costs once it has paid the full $100,000 in damages.

Coverage E protection applies in all of the following locations:

- Anywhere the insured is found liable for bodily injury or property damage resulting from actions that have no business relation
- Residences acquired after the commencement of the policy period
- Property listed in the declarations section
- Property rented by the insured for non-business uses
- Temporary residences acquired by the insured
- Land on which the insured is building a new residence
- Vacant land in the insured's possession (owned or rented)
- Burial vaults/cemetery plots

Coverage F—Medical Payments to Others is a type of liability coverage available on all homeowner's policies. It covers **bodily injuries** sustained in the following situations:

- The injured party is staying at an insured location with permission from the insured.
- The injured party is not staying at an insured location, but the injury is caused by one of the following: an accident on insured property, a residence employee, or an animal in the insured's care or possession. Injuries occurring on a property adjacent to the insured property are also covered.

Coverage F reimburses any necessary medical expenses up to three years after the injury has occurred. There is a minimum limit of $1,000 per person. This coverage is applicable even when the insured is not liable for the injury. Coverage F does not cover injuries to the insured or his residents unless they are resident employees.

Coverages E and F exclude damages and injuries from liability coverage if they result from or involve any of the following:

- An action the insured expects or intends
- Business-related acts or pursuits
- A rented portion of the insured property, unless the rented portion is serving as a residence
- War or similar acts

21

- Communicable diseases transmitted by the insured
- Physical or mental abuse, including corporal punishment and sexual molestation
- Use, sale, or possession of controlled substances, except when these activities involve the legitimate and legal use of prescription drugs.
- Possession, use, maintenance, or loading/unloading of watercraft (in most cases), aircraft, and motor vehicles

Under certain circumstances, Coverages E and F will extend liability protection to watercraft. These circumstances include the following:

- The watercraft is in storage.
- The watercraft is less than 26 feet long, or is greater than 26 feet long and not owned or rented by the insured.
- The watercraft is a non-sailing vessel with 50 or less horsepower, and is not owned by the insured, or the watercraft is a non-sailing vessel with greater than 50 horsepower, and is not owned or rented by the insured.
- The watercraft is a non-sailing vessel with one or more outboard motors/engines outputting a total of 25 or less horsepower. Or, it is a non-sailing vessel with one or more outboard motors/engines outputting greater than 25 horsepower and the engines/motors are not owned by the insured. Or, it is a non-sailing vessel with outboard engines/motors outputting greater than 25 horsepower, and the engines/motors are owned by the insured. In this case, protection is provided as long as the engines/motors were acquired during or before the policy period.

Coverage E excludes the following liabilities from coverage:

- Damage to property that the insured owns, uses, or maintains
- Property damage or bodily injury already covered by Nuclear Energy Liability policies
- Cost of loss assessments required by property owners' associations or corporations of which the insured is a member
- Liabilities already covered under other contracts and agreements, unless the loss involves the insured location or the contract covered the liability of others before the occurrence

Coverage F excludes the following liabilities:

- Bodily injuries resulting from nuclear reactions and radiation exposure
- Residence employees who suffer bodily injuries (if the injury is not the result of the employee's work duties for the insured and is not sustained at the insured location)

ADDITIONAL LIABILITY COVERAGES

Claim expenses pays back defense costs, post judgment interest, lost bond premiums, and any other reasonable expenses the insured may incur at the insurer's request.

First aid expenses pays back any costs the insured may have incurred when rendering first aid during an accident.

Damage to property of others provides a maximum of $1,000 per occurrence when the insured damages or destroys property, even if he is not legally liable. This coverage applies to property rented or borrowed by the insured, but not property owned by the insured.

Loss assessment provides a maximum of $1,000 so the insured can pay his portion of any loss assessment required by a property owners' association or corporation during the policy period. This coverage does not apply unless the loss occurrence is included under the liability section of the policy or the liability is incurred by a director, officer, or trustee of the insured.

SECTION I (PROPERTY INSURANCE) ENDORSEMENTS

Section I (property insurance) endorsements offer additional coverage for the following types of property:

- cameras, films, and various projection equipment
- golf equipment
- postage stamps
- coins
- fine arts
- jewelry
- furs and similar clothing
- silverware

Under the **scheduled personal property** endorsement, the insured can schedule a separate insurance amount for each of the above property types. This endorsement provides open peril protection, carries no deductible, and reimburses losses at actual cash value, market value, repair or replacement cost, or value basis.

The **personal property replacement cost** endorsement reimburses losses at replacement cost. Consequently, certain items are excluded from this endorsement, such as antiques and rare paintings.

Permitted incidental occupancies endorsement eliminates many of the exclusions that deny or limit insurance to residence-based businesses. **Earthquake** endorsement covers earthquake damage to personal property. **Home day care coverage** endorsement provides coverage for home day care businesses.

SECTION II (LIABILITY INSURANCE) ENDORSEMENTS

Watercraft endorsement provides liability coverage for the following:

- Watercraft equal to or less than 26 feet in length with outboard engines/motors outputting greater than 25 horsepower and watercraft with inboard or inboard-outboard engines/motors
- Sailboats longer than 26 feet in length

Business pursuits endorsement covers businesses activities performed off of the premises of the residence, while personal injury endorsement expands bodily injury coverage to include personal injury.

Limited fungi, wet or dry rot, or bacteria endorsement is only available for HO-3 and HO-5 policies, and is offered on both Section I (property) and Section II (liability) of homeowner's insurance. As a Section I endorsement, it covers the following costs: all losses caused by mold if the loss was a product of a covered peril, removing mold, and removing and replacing portions of the insured property in order to treat the mold. As a Section II endorsement, it covers damages resulting from actual, alleged, or threatened mold contact.

EARTHQUAKE INSURANCE AND MOBILE HOME INSURANCE

Earthquake insurance can be offered either as an endorsement on dwelling and homeowner's policies or as a separate policy. It insures structures and their contents against damage caused by earthquakes and their aftershocks. According to the policy, a single earthquake occurrence includes the initial tremor and any aftershock for the next 72 hours.

Mobile home insurance covers the following:

- The mobile home unit itself, including any built-in equipment
- Any equipment or structure that is attached but not originally built-in, such as carports, water pumps, shelters, etc.
- Various living expenses
- Collision damage while the mobile home is being moved (This is an optional coverage.)
- Homeowner liability, much like Section II of the homeowner's policy

Mobile home insurance can be acquired as a **separate package policy**, an endorsement on dwelling policies, or an endorsement on homeowner's policies (HO-2 or HO-3).

DWELLING INSURANCE

Dwelling insurance is a personal, mono-line (property only) policy intended for people who rent property to others, own seasonal/vacation dwellings, or own dwellings whose risk level is too high for other types of policies, such as homeowner's insurance. Dwelling insurance covers the following types of property:

- Dwellings housing no more than four families or apartments housing no more than five boarders
- Private outbuildings that are part of uninsured property
- Mobile homes at fixed locations (on a permanent foundation)
- Vacant dwellings
- Personal property contained in eligible dwellings

Although dwelling insurance is not intended for farm or commercial coverage, it can be used for incidental businesses and professional offices that are oriented towards service rather than sales. Businesses are incidental if they have only one or two people working at any given time. Dwelling insurance includes three different policy types: **basic form (DP-1)**, **broad form (DP-2)**, and **special form (DP-3)**. Each form gives progressively more coverage than the last.

All dwelling insurance policy forms include the following coverages:

- **Coverage A—dwelling**: This insures the dwelling, all attached structures (additions such as garages), fixtures, doors, windows, and all materials, supplies, or equipment used to build, maintain, or service the property.
- **Coverage C—personal property**: This covers the personal property of the insured and anyone else living in the dwelling, including family members, guests, and servants. The property must be usual to the dwelling, and certain types of property are excluded, including animals, aircraft, motor vehicles, any boats other than rowboats and canoes, business equipment and records, and financial items (money, coins, bank notes, deeds, evidence of debt, etc.). Coverage C also includes an **automatic removal coverage** provision, which protects property as it is being moved to a new location.

The insured is not required to purchase the above coverages, even though they are preprinted on the dwelling policy form.

All dwelling insurance policy forms include the following coverages:

- **Coverage B—other (appurtenant) structures**: This insures all structures that are part of the property but detached from the dwelling (though they may be connected by a utility line).
- **Coverage D—fair rental value**: This covers any losses in rent payments resulting from property damage. Assume, for example, that Mike is renting a room from Joe. If the room is damaged and rendered uninhabitable, Joe can no longer collect rent from Mike, but Joe is reimbursed the rent payment under Coverage D. This coverage even applies when damage to a separate adjacent property renders the insured property uninhabitable. Under this condition, the time period over which reimbursement payments are made cannot exceed two weeks.

The insured is not required to purchase the above coverages, even though they are preprinted on the dwelling policy form.

The **dwelling property basic form**, or **DP-1**, automatically protects against the following named perils: **fire, lightning,** and **internal explosions**. The policy does not cover steam explosions caused by equipment that is leased, operated, or owned by the insured. The insured can also purchase **extended coverage**, or **EC**, against the following perils:

- Windstorm or hail
- Explosion (external, internal, and explosions that occur at adjacent properties)
- Civil commotion (rioting and looting)
- Volcanic eruption
- Aircraft contact with the dwelling
- Vehicle contact with the dwelling (unless the vehicle is owned or operated by the insured)
- Smoke (except for fireplaces and agricultural or industrial sources)
- Vandalism and malicious mischief, or V&MM (except for glass damage, theft, and situations in which the building has been left vacant for 31 or more consecutive days)

DP-1 forms automatically provide Coverages A, B, C, and D, as well as **other coverages**. They can also include Coverage E via endorsement.

Coverage E—additional living expenses covers the insured's living expenses if his property is damaged and rendered uninhabitable. Dining, motel, laundry, and transportation expenses are reimbursed until the insured's property is repaired or he is able to relocate to a permanent dwelling. Coverage E also applies when the insured property is made uninhabitable because of damage to a neighboring area. In this situation, however, payments can only be issued for a maximum of two weeks.

Dwelling policy forms include the following **other coverages**:

- **Debris removal** – This reimburses the cost of removing debris left behind as a result of an insurable loss.
- **Property removed** (or **removal coverage**) – This applies when property is being moved to an alternate location for the purposes of protecting it from a covered peril. DP-1 forms cover the property for a maximum of five days. DP-2 and DP-3 forms cover the property for up to 30 days.

Dwelling policy forms include the following **other coverages**:

- **Worldwide coverages** – This covers personal property (up to a maximum of 10% of the Coverage C limit) no matter where in the world it is located.
- **Improvements, alterations, and additions** – This insures tenants who are making improvements or alterations to a rented dwelling at their own expense. If a covered loss occurs, this coverage provides 10% of the Coverage C limit.
- **Reasonable repairs** – This covers any reasonable repairs that may be required after a covered peril has damaged the property.
- **Fire department service charge** – This provides $500 for fire department charges. The insurer will owe this amount if he must call the fire department to protect against a covered peril.

Other structures insure buildings that are appurtenant to the dwelling, and provide a maximum reimbursement amount of 10% of Coverage A's limit. For instance, consider a dwelling worth $150,000 with an appurtenant maintenance shed worth $15,000. The full value of the shed would be covered by other structures because 10% of $150,000 is $15,000. Although other structures is very similar to Coverage B, the two are completely separate. In fact, the insured does not need to purchase additional insurance under Coverage B unless the appurtenant structure's total value exceeds 10% of Coverage A's limit. For example, if the above shed were worth $25,000, the insured would need to purchase an additional $10,000 under Coverage B to cover the shed's full value. Under DP-1, other structures are covered under Coverage A. Consequently, any amount used to insure appurtenant structures is deducted from dwelling coverage. Under DP-2 and DP-3, this coverage is part of additional insurance. It is not deducted from dwelling coverage.

RENTAL VALUE

Rental value reimburses rent payments that are lost when damage to a rental property renders it uninhabitable. The insured is reimbursed the lost rent. The total reimbursements cannot exceed 10% of Coverage A's limit. The entire amount is not paid out in one installment. Instead, it is distributed at a rate of $1/12^{th}$ of the maximum amount for each month the property cannot be used. Consider, for instance, a rental dwelling with a maximum insurable limit of $240,000 under Coverage A. The rental value coverage for this property would be $24,000 (10% of $240,000). If the property is damaged and the tenants are forced to leave, the insured would receive rental insurance at a rate of $2,000 per month ($1/12^{th}$ of $24,000). Although very similar to Coverage D, rental value is a completely different coverage. Under DP-1, rental value is part of Coverage A, and is therefore deducted from available dwelling coverage. Under DP-2 and DP-3, this coverage is part of additional insurance, and is not deducted from dwelling coverage.

EXCLUSIONS UNDER DP-1

The **DP-1 (dwelling property basic form)** excludes these coverages:

- The cost of replacing existing materials with more expensive materials when the replacement is mandated by new laws or ordinances (unless the insured is replacing regular glass with safety glass)
- Damage from water seepage or leaks
- Earthquake damage (except fire or explosion damage caused by the earthquake)
- Intentional damage by either the insured or a person acting under the direction of the insured
- War-related damage
- Nuclear hazard-related damage
- Any damage incurred as a result of the insured failing to protect his property when it was in imminent danger (especially following a loss)
- Damage from power loss if the loss was caused somewhere other than the insured's property

PERILS AND LOSSES COVERED UNDER DP-2

The **dwelling property broad form**, or **DP-2**, automatically covers the following perils:

- Weight of sleet, ice, or snow against the roof and exterior walls
- Damage caused by burglars (excluding theft)
- Falling objects
- Sudden and accidental discharge or overflow of water or steam
- Sudden and accidental damage from artificial electrical current
- Sudden and accidental cracking, burning, or tearing apart of any water, steam, or air system
- Freezing of sprinkler system, plumbing, heating, air conditioning, or other household appliances
- All regular and EC perils covered under DP-1

Smoke protection includes fireplace smoke, and vehicle impact protection includes driveways, walkways, and fences. Vehicular damage to the dwelling and appurtenant structures is protected, even if the driver is one of the insureds. DP-2 forms automatically include Coverages A, B, C, D, and E. They provide all **other coverages** found in DP-1, as well as a few additional **other coverages**.

OTHER COVERAGES THAT ARE EXCLUSIVE TO DP-2 AND DP-3

The following **other coverages** are only provided by DP-2 and DP-3:

- **Collapse** – covers damage caused by building collapse
- **Trees, shrubs, and other plants** – This insures against damage to trees, shrubs, and other plants. The coverage amount cannot exceed 5% of Coverage A's limit, or $500 for a single plant.
- **Glass or safety glazing material** – insures against glass breakage, glazing material breakage, and any damage caused by such breakage
- **Ordinance or law** – reimburses any cost increases caused by the passage of new laws and ordinances regulating the repair, renovation, or demolition of damaged property (as long as the damage was caused by a covered peril)

PERILS AND LOSSES COVERED UNDER DP-3

The **dwelling policy special form**, or **DP-3**, automatically provides **open peril** protection on Coverages A and B (the dwelling and all appurtenant structures) and **named peril** protection on Coverage C (personal property). Open peril contracts cover any risk of physical loss, unless the risk has been excluded in the contract. DP-3 forms exclude the following risks:

- Exclusions already listed under the exclusion section of DP-1 forms
- Water or ice damage to pavements, patios, fences, foundations, etc.
- Damage from constant water or steam seepage/leakage
- Damage from pollutants
- Wind, hail, ice, snow, and sleet damage to antenna assemblies and lawns
- Damage from freezing water, heating, and air systems, unless the insured took reasonable care to avoid freezing
- Gradual and natural deterioration (mold, corrosion, etc.)
- Collapse, except those situations listed under **other coverages**
- Damage from domestic animals, birds, vermin, and insects
- Theft and **V&MM** when the dwelling is under construction or has been vacant for 31 or more days
- Cracking of pavement, foundations, walls, roofs, floors, and ceilings

SETTLING LOSSES USING DP-2 AND DP-3 FORMS

DP-2 and DP-3 forms outline specific methods of reimbursement for different types of loss. When the loss involves personal property, the insured is reimbursed the **actual cash value** (**ACV**). When the loss involves a dwelling or other structure, however, the insured is paid the **replacement cost**. Depreciation will not be deducted from the amount paid out as long as the insured has purchased a policy covering at least 80% of the replacement value of the structure at the time of the loss. If the policy does not meet or exceed the 80% limit, the insured is reimbursed the ACV or the proportional replacement cost, whichever represents the greater value. These values are calculated as follows:

- Insurance Coverage Amount / 80% of Full Replacement Cost = Proportional Replacement Cost Percentage
- PRC Percentage x Loss Amount = Proportional Replacement Cost

Assume, for example, that a person owns a dwelling with a $100,000 replacement value, but only purchases $40,000 worth of insurance. If a $20,000 loss occurs, the proportional replacement cost would be calculated as follows:

- $40,000 / $80,000 = 50%
- 0.50 x $20,000 = $10,000

CONDITIONS FOUND ON DWELLING POLICIES

In addition to **the pair or set condition**, **other insurance condition**, and **recovered property condition**, dwelling policies have the following settlement conditions:

- **Loss payment condition** – Upon reaching a settlement amount with the insured, an insurer must distribute payment within 30 days.
- **Our option condition** – For up to 30 days after receiving a statement of loss from the insured, the insurer has the right to repair or replace damaged property with comparable property.

- **Loss settlement condition** – Although every covered property loss must be assessed at actual cash value (ACV), it cannot surpass the repair or replacement cost.
- **Deductible clause** – The insurer is only obligated to pay the loss amount over the deductible up to the limit of liability, which represents the maximum possible amount. This settlement condition is considered a clause because it is included in the declaration section rather than the conditions section.

LIMITED THEFT COVERAGE

Limited theft coverage can be added as an endorsement to dwelling policies. It insures against theft of personal property, but only covers property stored on the premises and property owned by occupants of the dwelling who are not owners, such as tenants. It protects against theft, attempted theft, and vandalism and malicious mischief (V&MM) as long as the building has not been vacant for 31 or more consecutive days. Limited theft coverage includes the following sublimits:

- $1,000 on watercraft, including equipment and trailers
- $1,000 on other types of trailers
- $2,000 on firearms

This policy excludes the following kinds of property: precious metals; money; securities; jewelry; silverware; watches; furs; animals, birds, and fish; motor vehicles and related equipment; credit cards; property in the mail; property in the custody of a bailee; an employee's business property; aircraft (excluding models and hobby aircraft); sample and sale property; tenant property if the tenant is not related to the insured; property insured by other insurance.

BROAD THEFT COVERAGE

Broad theft coverage can be added as an endorsement to dwelling policies, but is reserved for the dwelling's owner-occupant. It insures against theft of personal property, and protects against the same perils found in limited theft coverage. It covers property found on and off the premises, but coverage for property found off the premises may have different liability limits. Broad theft coverage includes the following sublimits:

- $1,000 on watercraft, including equipment and trailers
- $1,000 on other types of trailers
- $2,000 on firearms
- $2,500 on silverware, pewterware, and goldware
- $200 on money and precious metals
- $1,000 on securities, manuscripts, and similar property
- $1,000 for jewelry, watches, precious stones, and furs

With the exception of precious metals, money, securities, jewelry, silverware, watches, and furs, broad theft coverage excludes the same types of property as limited theft coverage.

COVERAGES L AND M

Coverage L—Personal Liability can be acquired as an endorsement. It covers the insured against personal liability damages for which he may be responsible, such as the types of bodily injury and property damage included under the policy. In addition, the insurance company pays to defend the insured against lawsuits, including fraudulent ones. Personal liability coverage has a minimum limit of $100,000.

Coverage M—Medical Payment to Others is also an endorsement. It reimburses any medical expenses resulting from the following situations:

- A person is injured while staying on the insured's property with permission from the insured.
- A person is injured off the insured's property as a result of the insured's activities, a situation at the insured's property, or the insured's animal(s).

The Coverage M endorsement does not cover injuries to the insured or his family. However, it does apply to situations in which the insured is not liable. The minimum coverage limit is $1,000 per person. Coverages L and M include the following additional coverages: **damage to others' property, claims expenses,** and **others' first aid expenses**. When the insured damages the property of others, the insurer provides a maximum reimbursement of $500 per occurrence. First aid expenses are only covered when they involve a bodily injury covered under the policy.

Coverages L and M also reimburse the following covered claims expenses:

- The insured's court costs if the suit is covered under the policy
- Defense costs
- Post judgment interest on settlements
- Bond premiums if the bond is needed as part of the insured's legal defense and the premium does not surpass Coverage L's limit
- Expenses incurred due to requests by the insurer that are intended to facilitate claim investigation or defense are reimbursed. The daily limit for lost earnings is $50.

Coverages L and M exclude coverage for losses resulting from the following:

- War
- Communicable diseases transmitted by the insured
- The insured's business activities and decisions
- Sexual, physical, and mental abuse, including corporal punishment
- Losses that the insured expects or intentionally creates
- Damage to a premise that is not part of the insured location
- Damage to a premise that is ineligible for coverage
- Use of controlled substances, other than the legal use of prescription drugs
- Damage to most types of watercraft, aircraft, and vehicles

Automatic increase in insurance is an endorsement available on dwelling policies. It provides annual increases (4%, 6%, or 8%) in insurance coverage.

Dwelling under construction is also a dwelling policy endorsement. It covers a partially completed dwelling when the named insured is the intended occupant.

Coverage L does not provide reimbursement for the following losses:

- Losses already protected by laws such as Workers' Compensation
- Losses that a corporation or association levies against the insured
- Property damage, if the property is owned by the insured
- Property damage, if the insured is renting, occupying, or using the property

- Losses that are already covered by other insurance
- Injuries sustained by the insured or any family members or minors living in the insured's household

Coverage M excludes the following injures from coverage:

- Nuclear hazard-related injuries
- Injuries to people who reside in the insured dwelling but are not residence employees
- Injuries to residence employees if the injuries are sustained off the insured property and are not related to work performed on the insured property

COMMERCIAL PACKAGE POLICY (CPP)

A **commercial package policy**, or **CPP**, provides mono-line and multi-line coverage for businesses. It consists of a common policy declarations section, a common policy conditions section, and two or more of the following coverages: commercial property, commercial general liability, commercial crime, commercial auto, commercial inland marine, farm, employment practices liability, professional liability, and boiler and machinery. In a CPP, the **common policy declarations** section provides the following information:

- Named insured's identity and mailing address
- Policy period
- Description of the business being covered
- List of coverages purchased, including their premium amounts
- Types of forms necessary for coverage

In most cases, a CPP also includes **interline endorsements**, which can be applied to multiple insurance lines. These endorsements can be optional or required under the policy.

The **common policy conditions** section lays out the responsibilities and obligations of the **first named insured** on the policy. These responsibilities may include premium payments, cancellation notices, policy term changes, book and record examinations, inspections and surveys, and transfer of rights and duties, all of which fall solely on the insured named first in the declarations section.

The **cancellation condition** explains the procedures for canceling policies. Policies must be cancelled in writing by the first named insured, who will receive any premium refund. The insurance company can only cancel the policy for the specific reasons outlined in the policy, and must send a written notice to the first named insured's last known address. Canceling due to nonpayment of premiums requires 10 days notice, while canceling due to any other reason requires 30 days notice.

According to the **premium condition**, the first named insured is accountable for paying premiums and receiving premium refunds.

According to the **changes condition**, only the first named insured can change policy terms, provided he receives permission and an endorsement from the insurer.

The **examination of your books and records condition** empowers the insurer to audit the insured's books and records. An audit can be done at any time during the policy period or during the three years following the policy period's conclusion.

The **inspection and surveys condition** empowers the insurer to survey and inspect the insured's business for reasons related to premiums and insurability (not safety). Inspections can be conducted at any time, and the insurer can recommend changes.

According to the **transfer of your rights and duties under this policy condition**, the insured cannot transfer his rights and duties to any party unless he obtains written consent from the insurer. The only exception to this condition is if the insured dies, in which case his rights and duties are transferred to a legal representative.

EARTHQUAKE AND VOLCANIC ERUPTION, AND SPOILAGE ENDORSEMENTS

The **earthquake and volcanic eruption endorsement** can be added to cause of loss forms. It insures commercial property against damage caused by volcanic eruption, explosion, or effusion, lava, ash, or airborne shockwaves, and earth movement. For insurance purposes, a single instance of earthquake or volcanic eruption includes the initial shock or eruption and any proceeding shock or eruption over the next 168 hours. At the insured's request, coverage for this endorsement can be limited to sprinkler leakage (**earthquake—sprinkler leakage**).

Spoilage endorsement is available on both the building and personal property coverage form and condominium commercial unit-owners coverage form, and covers the insured's perishable stock, which is defined as personal property that will spoil unless it is kept in a controlled environment.

VALUE REPORTING AND ORDINANCE OR LAW COVERAGE ENDORSEMENTS

The **value reporting endorsement** is intended for property that is subject to regular changes in value, as well as property that is occasionally moved between locations, such as business personal property, others' personal property, and stock. This endorsement relies on a **value reporting form**, which the insured uses to report the actual value of his property at a specific time and location. These values are reported at regular intervals, and are used to determine the premium payments and insurance amounts. Coverage will vary depending on risk at a specific location, and the insured normally carries more insurance than they need. The **peak season endorsement**, which is a type of value reporting form, allows the insured to have a higher amount of coverage at different times during the year.

The **ordinance or law coverage endorsement** protects the insured when his loss amount is increased by ordinances and laws. This endorsement applies specifically to demolition costs, construction costs, and value loss to undamaged buildings.

COVERAGE A ON BUSINESS OWNER'S POLICIES

Coverage A—buildings covers the following types of property:

- Buildings and structures located on the premises
- Machinery and equipment that is permanently installed
- Completed additions
- Indoor and outdoor fixtures (lawnmowers, garden hoses, etc.)
- Personal property that the insured provides in rooms and common areas
- Personal property necessary to repair and maintain buildings and structures on the premises (refrigeration equipment, kitchen equipment, fire extinguishers, coverings, etc.)
- Incomplete additions (if they are not already covered by other insurance)

- Repairs and alterations (if they are not already covered by other insurance)
- Equipment, temporary structures, and materials that are used for repairs, alterations, or maintenance that are located within 100 feet of the premises (if they are not already covered by other insurance)

COVERAGE B ON BUSINESS OWNER'S POLICIES

Coverage B—business personal property covers the following classes of personal property:

- Business property used and owned by the insured
- Others' property being held or controlled by the insured
- Tenant improvements and betterments, including additions, installations, alterations, and fixtures (These must be acquired and permanently attached at the owner's expense, and it must be unlawful to remove them)
- Exterior building glass, which must be owned by the insured or under his care (This coverage is intended for insureds, who are also tenants, without building coverage)
- Leased personal property that the insured is contractually obligated to insure, such as rented photocopiers and rented computer equipment

Coverage B protects personal property located within the building, on the premises, or within 100 feet of the premises, either in a vehicle or outside.

PROPERTY NOT COVERED UNDER BUSINESS OWNER'S POLICIES

BOPs do not cover the following property:

- Aircraft
- Watercraft and its equipment when they are on the water
- Vehicles requiring motor vehicle registration
- Computers that are permanently installed in motor vehicles
- Bills, accounts, food stamps, evidences of debt, and other monetary papers and records
- Outdoor fences, shrubs, plants, and trees, unless they are part of additional coverages
- Illegally transported property and other contraband
- Land, water, lawns, and crops
- Money/securities, unless they are part of additional coverages
- Outdoor signs detached from structures, unless they are part of additional coverages
- Outdoor antennas (radio and television), satellite dishes, and their equipment (wiring, masts, towers, etc.), unless they are part of additional coverages

BUSINESS OWNER'S POLICIES

Business owner's policies, or BOPs, are multi-line, commercial package policies intended for certain types of businesses, usually those with a single location and standard coverage needs. In fact, a business is not eligible for BOP coverage unless its type is specifically identified by ISO and it conforms to certain occupancy and size restrictions. The following types of property and businesses are completely excluded from coverage:

- Most types of auto repair and service stations
- Amusement parks
- Garages and parking lots
- Auto, motorcycle, and motor/mobile home dealerships
- Bars/pubs

33

- Banks, S&Ls, and other financial institutions
- Buildings used for manufacturing
- Manufacturing businesses
- Condominium associations (except condominiums used for offices or residences)
- Household personal property
- Most types of one- or two-family dwellings

A BOP is a single form containing property coverage (Coverage A and Coverage B), liability coverage, policy conditions, policy declarations, and optional coverages.

BOP OCCUPANCY AND SIZE RESTRICTIONS ON COMMERCIAL PROPERTIES

The following commercial properties can receive BOP coverage only if they conform to certain occupancy and size restrictions:

- **Apartments**, including **residential condominium associations** – Coverage is available for buildings of any size, personal property, and permitted occupancies such as offices, mercantile, processing, eligible wholesaler, and service.
- **Motels** – Coverage is available for buildings less than three stories high, personal property, bars/cocktail lounges, and seasonal operations closed for 30 days or less.
- **Offices**, including **office condominium associations** – Coverage is available for buildings less than 7 stories high that are less than 100,000 square feet, business personal property contained in offices covering 25,000 square feet or less in a single building, and permitted occupancies such as mercantile, processing, eligible wholesaler, service, and contractors.
- **Wholesale risks** – Coverage is available for buildings whose availability to the public is limited to 25% or less of its total floor area, personal property, and a maximum of 25% of the gross sales from retail operations.

The following commercial properties can receive BOP coverage only if they conform to certain occupancy and size restrictions:

- **Condominium commercial unit-owners** – Coverage is available for business personal property if the condominium is being used for the following occupancies: wholesaler, processing, office, service, contractor, and eligible mercantile.
- **Mercantile risks** – Coverage is available for eligible buildings and personal property.
- **Processing and service risks** – Coverage is available for select processing risks, select service risks, and a maximum of 25% of the gross annual sales generated off-premises.
- **Self-storage facilities** – Coverage is available for buildings less than three stories high and personal property. Coverage is not available for facilities providing cold storage or industrial waste storage.

COVERAGE PROVIDED BY BUSINESS OWNER'S POLICIES AND THE THEFT COVERAGE PROVIDED BY BOPS

In most cases, BOPs provide open peril coverage. With the appropriate endorsement, however, BOPs can offer named peril coverage that only protects against the following types of loss:

- Lightning
- Fire
- Windstorm and hail
- Smoke
- Explosion

- Vandalism
- Riots/civil commotion
- Aircraft and other vehicles
- Volcanic eruption
- Leaking fire extinguishers and their equipment
- Sinkholes
- Water damage
- Weight of ice, sleet, and snow
- Falling objects

BOPs offer a maximum coverage limit of $2,500 when the following types of property are stolen: garments made of or lined with fur; dies, patterns, molds, and forms; jewelry worth $100 or more per item; watches worth $100 or more per item; precious/semiprecious stones, precious metals, and bullion.

COVERAGE LIMITATIONS ON BUSINESS OWNER'S POLICIES

Steam equipment (boilers, pipes, turbines, etc.) and **water heating equipment** (hot water boilers, etc.) are not covered when they are damaged by internal problems inherent in the equipment. However, they are covered if the damage is caused by gas or fuel explosions within the furnace or ducts that convey gas.

Missing property is not covered if there is no physical evidence showing why the loss occurred. The only exceptions are money and securities, for which optional coverage is available.

Property being transferred beyond the covered premises without permission is not covered.

The **building interior** is covered when it is damaged by rain, sleet, ice, sand, or dust only if they entered through a hole in an exterior wall or roof that was created by a covered peril.

Fragile articles, such as marbles, glassware, porcelains, and chinaware, are only covered when damaged by losses specifically named under the policy.

BOP EXCLUSIONS RELATED TO PERILS EXTERNAL TO A BUSINESS

Business owner's policies exclude losses from coverage if they result from the following types of external perils:

- Earth movement
- Water damage, such as floods, mudslides, seepage, and sewer backup
- Natural wear and tear
- Animals such as insects, birds, and rodents
- Smog
- Expansion, contraction, settling, and cracking
- Contributing weather conditions
- Certain types of corrosion such as rust, decay, fungus, and other innate defects
- Industrially or agriculturally generated smoke, gas, or vapor
- Rain, sleet, snow, and ice when it damages personal property left outside
- Loss or delay of market or use
- War/military endeavors
- Nuclear-related damage
- Law changes

- Types of collapse that are not protected under the policy
- Pollution, except in cases where it results from a covered peril

Power outage due to a failure at a utility service beyond the insured premises, unless the outage damages computers and electronic media

Business owner's policies exclude losses from coverage if they result from the following types of internal perils:

- Computers failing to acknowledge dates and times
- Steam boiler, engine, pipe, or turbine explosion
- Artificial electric current, unless it is generated within 100 feet of the insured premises
- Freezing that causes leakage of water, powder, liquids, or molten material from fire protective systems, unless the insured took appropriate measures to protect the system
- The insured's employees engaging in criminal or dishonest behavior
- Being tricked or swindled into giving up property
- Poor planning, design, workmanship, etc.
- Failure to make decisions in a timely or appropriate manner
- Failure to preserve existing property after a loss has already occurred
- Erasure of electronic media by electrical or magnetic sources
- Poor design, installation, maintenance, repair, or modification of computer and other systems
- Mistakes in programming, data storage, or processing/copying of papers and records

ADDITIONAL COVERAGES ON BUSINESS OWNER'S POLICIES

Debris removal reimburses the cost of removing debris, provided its presence was caused by a covered loss. To receive this coverage, the insured must submit an accident report within 180 days of the loss or the conclusion of the policy period. In most cases, debris removal has a maximum payout of 25% of the amount reimbursed for the direct physical loss plus the deductible. The insurer's total payout for the direct physical loss and debris removal cannot exceed the applicable insurance limit. However, the insurer may provide an extra $10,000 over the policy limit (per occurrence) if the following conditions are present:

- The insurance limit is insufficient to cover the cost of direct physical loss and debris removal.
- The maximum limit on debris removal is insufficient to reimburse the cost of debris removal.

A **collapse** occurs when a building is rendered uninhabitable because all or a portion of it has fallen down. This coverage insures against collapses that result from the following: building glass breakage, weight of people/personal property, weight of rain, and insect/vermin damage if the insured was unaware of the damage before the collapse occurred. A collapse is also covered when it occurs **during** construction or renovation due to poor quality building materials. Certain outdoor properties (such as gutters, awnings, yard fixtures, swimming pools and related equipment, piers, docks, retaining walls, and various paved surfaces) are also covered if they are directly damaged by a building collapse. This coverage applies to collapsed personal property if the following criteria are present:

- The personal property is within the insured building.
- One of the causes listed above leads to the collapse.
- The personal property is not one of the outdoor items listed above.

Business income reimburses the insured for income he loses when his business is forced to cease operations. This coverage only applies if the cessation was caused by direct physical damage to business property located on or within 100 feet of the insured premises. Additionally, the damage must have resulted from a covered peril. While the property is being repaired, the policy covers any income losses incurred within the 12 months directly following the day the damage occurred. Depending on the circumstances of the loss, this coverage may offer **extended business income coverage**, which continues to issue payments even after business operations have resumed. The insured will receive payments until his previous earning level is restored, or until a condition outlined in the declarations section is met. Business income coverage is paid out independent of the limits of insurance.

Extra expense applies when business operations are threatened by a covered loss. For a 12-month period immediately following the loss, this coverage reimburses money that the insured must spend in order to avoid or reduce suspension of business operations. Reimbursements are made in addition to the limits of insurance.

Increased cost of construction covers additional costs the insured may incur when a damaged building must be repaired in accordance with some ordinance or law. This coverage has a $10,000 limit, and only provides coverage for buildings insured at replacement cost. If the insured chooses to rebuild the damaged building at a new location rather than the old location, the reimbursement amount is limited to the increased cost of construction at the old location. However, if the ordinance or law mandates moving to a new location, the reimbursement amount will cover the increased cost of construction at the new location.

Civil authority applies when civil authorities are preventing the insured from accessing his property because a covered loss has damaged property at a location adjacent to the insured premises. This coverage reimburses any **business income** or **extra expense** losses incurred during the insured's absence from the covered property. For instance, assume that a fire is damaging a building adjacent to the insured's business. If the insured is denied access to his business because civil authorities fear the fire may spread, he is protected by civil authority coverage. Business income coverage begins 72 hours after civil authorities initially deny access to the property, and continues for a maximum of three consecutive weeks. Extra expenses are covered immediately following the denial of access. Coverage for extra expenses continues for three consecutive weeks or for the duration of the business income coverage, whichever is longer.

Forgery and alteration applies when someone forges or alters the insured's checks or similar documents. It covers any reasonable legal expenses incurred by the insured as a result of his refusal to pay for forged purchases or drafts. Coverage is limited to $2,500 or the limit shown in the declarations section.

Business income from dependent properties applies when damage to a dependent property results in income loss. A **dependent property** is defined as a business that assists the insured in the following ways: delivering materials, accepting the insured's goods, manufacturing goods that will be delivered to the insured's customers, or expanding the insured's customer base. The insurance limit cannot exceed $5,000 or the amount listed in the declaration section. Income loss coverage starts 72 hours after the loss event occurs, and lasts until the date the repairs should be completed.

Money orders and counterfeit paper currency covers the insured when he accepts counterfeit currency and/or money orders in exchange for goods and services. Coverage is limited to $1,000.

Water or other liquid, powder, or molten materials covers building damage when it is caused by indirect escape of these substances. It also covers the cost of removing and replacing the system from which the escape occurred if building damage is already covered by some other insurance. If the damage is caused by freezing or discharge from the automatic fire protection system, this coverage reimburses the cost of repairing or replacing damaged fire extinguisher equipment.

Pollutant clean up and removal covers the expense of removing or extracting pollutants from the insured's premises when they are placed there by a covered loss. Coverage is limited to $10,000 per 12-month policy period, and the loss must be reported within 180 days following the loss or 180 days before the end of the policy period, whichever represents the earlier date.

Fire extinguisher systems recharge expense covers the following costs:

- Recharging or replacing the insured's fire extinguishers and extinguisher systems
- Covered property damage resulting from accidental discharge of extinguisher systems

The coverage is limited to $1,000, and only applies if the system discharge occurred within 100 feet of the insured's premises.

Preservation of property applies when the insured moves property to a different location as a means of protecting it from a covered peril. This coverage lasts 30 days from the date of removal, and insures the property against direct physical damage by any cause of loss as it is being moved or stored.

Fire department service charge covers the charges and fees that may be incurred when the fire department is called upon to save or protect covered property. Coverage is limited to $1,000, and only applies when the insured is contractually or legally obligated to pay such a fee.

Glass expense applies when damaged glass cannot be repaired or replaced immediately. It reimburses the cost of boarding up and/or temporarily covering openings, as well as the cost of removing obstructions to the repair process.

COVERAGE EXTENSIONS ON BUSINESS OWNER'S POLICIES

Newly acquired or constructed property extends coverage to new buildings ($250,000 per location) and new business personal property ($100,000 per location). The duration of coverage is whichever of the following represents the shortest time period: 30 days from the date the property is acquired or construction begins, the remainder of the policy period, or the length of time before the insured reports new property values to the insurer.

Valuable papers and records coverage is an extension of business personal property coverage. It applies when the only existing copies of valuable papers and/or records are damaged, and covers the expenses of researching and restoring the lost data. The limit for damages occurring at the insured premises is $10,000 (or the amount listed in the declarations section), and the limit for damages occurring outside the insured premises is $5,000.

Personal effects coverage is an extension of business personal property coverage. It provides $2,500 per location for the personal effects of the insured and his employees.

Accounts receivable is another extension of business personal property coverage. It reimburses the following losses when they result from a covered loss:

- Customer payments that the insured is unable to collect
- Interest fees on loans intended to compensate for loss of customer payments
- Excess collection expenses
- Reasonable expenses needed to restore accounts receivable documents

There is a $10,000 limit for losses at the insured premises and a $5,000 limit for losses to accounts receivable outside the insured premises.

Outdoor property extension provides coverage for debris removal, as well as outdoor items such as fences, trees, plants, shrubs, freestanding signs, and radio, television, and satellite antennas/dishes. This coverage only protects against fire, explosion, riot/civil commotion, aircraft, and lightning, and has a maximum limit of $2,500 and $500 per shrub, tree, and plant.

Business property temporarily off the premises is covered if it is being moved to or stored at a location that is not owned or controlled by the insured. Coverage cannot exceed $5,000.

Additional coverages are part of existing coverages, and do not require additional premium payments. Optional coverages are separate from existing coverages, and do require additional premium payments.

OPTIONAL COVERAGE

Employee dishonesty covers personal property, money, and securities that are lost due to dishonest acts of an employee or employees working in collusion. Coverage does not apply if the insured and his partners were responsible for the dishonest acts, or if there is no evidence other than inventory or profit loss. In most cases, the policy only insures losses that occur during the policy period or the **discovery period**, which lasts for one year following policy termination. However, coverage for certain losses may extend beyond the discovery period under the following conditions:

- At the time the old policy was terminated, a new policy came into effect.
- If the new policy had been in effect when the loss occurred, it would have been covered under the new policy.

The maximum limit for employee dishonesty coverage is listed in the declarations section.

Mechanical breakdown insures against direct damage from the sudden and accidental breakdown of **objects**, which are defined as equipment falling under one of the following categories:

- Boiler/pressure vessels
- Air conditioning units

Coverage only applies if the object must be repaired or replaced and is owned by the insured or in his care or custody at the insured premises. Additionally, mechanical breakdown only covers accidents (as defined in the policy), and excludes any damage that occurs during object testing. If the insurance company finds the object is in an inherently unsafe or dangerous position, it may suspend coverage by notifying the insured in writing and sending a pro rata premium refund.

39

Outdoor signs are covered against direct physical damage or loss. These signs must be on the premises and must be either owned by the insured or in his care or custody. This coverage supersedes and replaces any other sign protection included in the policy, and has a maximum limit, which is stated in the declarations section.

Money and securities are covered against theft, destruction, or disappearance if they are used in the insured's business and stored within one of the following locations:

- Banks and savings institutions
- Insured premises
- Residence quarters of the insured, his partner, or his employees
- Another location while they are being moved between these locations

INTERNAL LIMIT AND INFLATION PROVISION

An **internal limit** (also known as an **inside limit**) is an insurance limit applied to each optional BOP coverage on a per occurrence basis. It is listed in the **limit of insurance provision**. Outdoor signs, fire department service charge, and pollutant removal/cleanup are examples of internal limits, which are offered in addition to the insurance limits of the policy. An **inflation provision** increases the insurance limits of the policy as the policy period moves forward. It is a percentage chosen by the insured.

BOPs include a separate $500 deductible for each of the following coverages:

- Building and business personal property (which is the base deductible)
- Optional coverages, including employee dishonesty, outdoor signs, and money and security
- Glass expenses additional coverages

LIABILITY COVERAGE

Under BOP liability coverage, the insurance company agrees to pay the insured's court costs when he is legally liable for property damage, bodily injury, and personal and advertising injury. The insurance company also has the right to investigate and settle claims. **Personal and advertising injury liability** may apply when the insured commits any of these offenses:

- Malicious prosecution
- False arrest or imprisonment
- Using the advertising ideas of another person
- Copyright/trade dress/slogan infringement
- Slandering or libeling a person or organization through oral and written publications
- Violating the right to privacy of another person
- Disparaging the goods and services of another person or organization
- Wrongfully evicting a person from his occupancy
- Wrongfully entering a person's occupancy
- Violating a person's right of private occupancy
- Consequential bodily injury

By making **supplementary payments**, the insured can increase the amount of liability coverage on business owner's policies. Supplementary payments include the following:

- Cost to release bond attachments
- Prejudgment interest

- Judgment interest that is assessed after the ruling has been made, but before it is paid in court
- $250 maximum for bail bonds arising from bodily injury liability coverage on vehicles
- Reasonable expenses paid by the insured as he assists the insurance company in investigating or defending liability suits (The insured pays these expenses at the insurance company's request.)
- Court costs paid by the insured during liability suits
- Expenses normally paid by the insurer
- Defense costs of an indemnitee, which is a party that provides goods and services for the insured, but is not insured under the policy (This payment is only available under certain conditions.)

With the exception of costs to release bond attachments, all supplementary coverages are offered in addition to the limits of the policy.

MEDICAL EXPENSES COVERAGE

Business owner's policies cover the following **medical expenses**, no matter who is at fault:

- Surgical costs
- Ambulance costs
- Hospital costs
- First aid rendered during the accident
- X-ray costs
- Nursing costs
- Dental costs
- Funeral costs

To receive coverage, these expenses must be necessitated due to a bodily injury sustained on or adjacent to the insured premises, or due to the insured's business operations. Additionally, the injured party must have been injured within the coverage territory during the policy period, and he must have reported the injury within a year of its occurrence. Because medical expenses coverage is intended for the general public, it usually excludes the following individuals from coverage: insured individuals; the insured's employees; people injured on a portion of the premises owned or rented and occupied by the insured; people injured during athletic exertions; people already covered by workers' compensation and comparable policies and laws.

EXCLUSIONS UNDER BOP LIABILITY COVERAGE

BOP liability excludes bodily injury and property damages from coverage when they result from the following:

- Expected or intentional injury, unless the insured is protecting himself using reasonable force
- Liquor-related activities, if the insured's business is involved in the sale, serving, or manufacturing of alcoholic beverages
- Injuries already covered by other contracts, workers' compensation, and other disability or benefit programs
- Bodily injury to the insured's employees during the regular course of their work
- Pollution
- Acts of war
- Aircraft, watercraft, or automobile ownership or maintenance

- Nuclear materials
- Loss of use, recall, repair, removal, disposal, etc. of the insured's work, goods, or property
- Rendering or failing to render professional services
- Damage to the insured's work or products
- Deficiency in or delay of the insured's products or work related to contract agreements

BOP liability excludes personal and advertising injury from coverage when they result from the following:

- Actions performed intentionally by the insured when he knows such actions will cause personal and advertising injury
- Oral and written statements made by the insured when he knows such statements are false
- Oral and written statements made before the policy period
- Actions for which the insured has contractually assumed liability
- Criminal actions by the insured
- Breach of contract
- Unauthorized inclusion of someone else's name or product in the insured's email, metatags, or domain
- Products and services of the insured that do not comply with quality standards
- Activities in electronic chat rooms or bulletin boards controlled by the insured
- False advertising of the insured's products and services
- Pollutant distribution or cleanup
- Activities of the insured's business related to advertising, broadcasting, and Internet search, content, or service

CATEGORIES OF INSUREDS ON BUSINESS OWNER'S POLICIES

BOP coverage applies to the following types of insureds:

- **Individual (sole proprietorship)** – includes named insured and his or her spouse
- **Partnership or joint venture** – includes named insured, his partners and members, and their spouses
- **Limited liability company** – includes named insured, his members, and his managers
- **Organizations other than those listed above** – includes name insured, executive officer and directors, and stockholders

Insureds only receive coverage when they are performing their respective job functions in the insured business. BOP coverage also extends to the following: the insured's employees (when performing their job functions); the insured's real estate manager (when acting in such a role); legal representatives who are given temporary custody of the insured's property following the insured's death; anyone operating the insured's mobile equipment with his permission.

CONDITIONS ON BUSINESS OWNER'S POLICIES

BOPs include **common policy conditions**, which are divided into two categories of property coverage (**property general conditions** and **property loss conditions**) and one category of liability coverage (**liability and medical expenses general conditions**). Property loss conditions place special limitations on the income reimbursement an insured can collect when electronic media and records are lost or damaged. Under these limitations, the insured is only covered for 60 consecutive days or the time necessary to repair or replace other property damaged during the same accident, whichever is longer. Under liability general conditions, policy coverage can be extended to meet any state's motor vehicle financial responsibility requirements. The insurer will provide any coverage necessary to fulfill state laws, such as liability, no-fault coverage, uninsured motorist, and underinsured motorist.

ENDORSEMENTS ON BUSINESS OWNER'S POLICIES

The **utility services—direct damage endorsement** insures against property damage or loss when it results from an interruption in utilities, such as water, communication, or power supply. This coverage only applies when the damaged property is covered by the policy and the utility service is interrupted by a covered loss.

Hired auto and non-owned auto liability endorsement provides liability coverage for bodily injury and property damage when they result from the following:

- The insured or his employees using or maintaining a hired auto while performing their work functions for the insured's business
- Any person using a non-owned auto while performing his work functions for the insured's business

When an auto is being used for the insured's business, but is not owned or rented by the insured, it is considered a **non-owned auto**. When an auto is leased, hired, or borrowed by the insured from someone other than his family or workers, it is a **hired auto**. The **utility services—time element endorsement** applies when utility services from a property outside the insured building are interrupted by a covered loss. This coverage reimburses lost business income and extra expenses.

According to the **protective safeguards endorsement**, the insurance company will only cover fire damage and other types of losses if the insured maintains the following protective safeguards:

- **P-1: automatic sprinkler system** – Includes all automatic fire protection systems, such as sprinklers, pipes, supervisory services, etc.
- **P-2: automatic fire alarm system** – Monitors the whole building and alerts some type of alarm station (central, public, or private)
- **P-3: security service** – Requires a guard to make hourly rounds during closing hours
- **P-4: service contract** – Obligates a private fire department to protect the premises
- **P-9** – Includes all other protective systems listed in the policy

BUSINESS INCOME COVERAGE FORMS

Business income coverage forms reimburse any business income the insured may lose when he is forced to suspend business operations due to direct physical damage from a covered peril. Business income includes two components: net income the business would have earned if it had not been forced to shut down, and the cost of maintaining normal business operations, which could include completing tasks like payroll. Coverage begins on the date of the loss and lasts until the date business operations should be restored. Business income forms are divided into two types:

- **Business income with extra expense**, which reimburses the specific expenses the insured may incur to avoid suspending business operations.
- **Business income without extra expense**, which provides **expense to reduce loss coverage** rather than extra expense coverage. The insured is reimbursed the money he spends to reduce the overall loss.

Both forms offer the following coverages: business income coverage including rental value coverage, business income coverage other than rental value coverage, and rental value coverage only.

43

Extended business income additional coverage extends the reimbursement period for loss of business income to 30 days after business operations have resumed.

Order of civil authority additional coverage reimburses loss of business income and extra expenses. It applies when civil authorities prevent the insured from entering his property because damage to another property has rendered the insured property uninhabitable.

Alterations and new buildings additional coverage also reimburses loss of business income and extra expense. It insures new buildings and alterations against covered losses. Coverage includes building materials, machinery, equipment, and supplies, provided they are used during construction, alteration, and occupancy of the building, and are located within 100 feet of the building. The coverage period begins on the date that business operations would have commenced if the damage had not occurred.

Extended period of indemnity optional coverage extends the reimbursement period for loss of business income to a certain number of days after business operations have resumed. This number of days, which can exceed the 30-day period under the extended business income additional coverage, is identified in the declarations section.

Maximum period of indemnity optional coverage states that reimbursement for extra expenses and loss of business income cannot exceed the total loss amount incurred during the first 120 days after the loss.

Under the **monthly limit of indemnity** optional coverage, the insured selects the amount he will be reimbursed for loss of business income for each 30-day period.

Agreed value optional coverage waives the coinsurance condition by requiring the insurer to carry an **agreed value** of insurance every 12 months. In order to establish the agreed value, the insured must submit a business income/report worksheet to the insurance company on an annual basis.

The **business income from dependent properties—broad form** covers direct physical loss to the following locations: contributing location, recipient location, manufacturing location, and lead location. A **contributing location** is the insured's sole supplier of raw materials and merchandise. A **recipient location** is the only business that purchases the insured's products. A **manufacturing location** is contracted by the insured to deliver his products. A **leader location** is a business that brings in customers for the insured. Each of the above business locations is separate from the insured's business. However, because damage or loss to these locations may cause the insured to suffer a loss of business income or earnings, he can seek coverage under the business income broad form.

Extra expense coverage forms are intended for businesses that simply cannot afford to suspend operations, such as newspapers, utility companies, and other businesses whose services or products are very important. This form does not provide loss of business income coverage. Instead, it only reimburses those costs that are necessary for the business to continue operations.

Insurance limits are expressed as percentages in the declarations section and assessed according to the period of restoration. Consider, for instance, a limit of 30%/70%/100%:

- For a restoration period of 30 days or less, the insurer pays 30% of the full insurance amount.
- For a restoration period of greater than 30 days, the insurer pays 70% of the full insurance amount.
- For a restoration period of greater than 60 days, the insurer pays 100% of the full insurance amount.

Legal liability coverage forms cover the insured when he is found legally liable for damage to property that is in his care but owned by someone else.

OCEAN MARINE INSURANCE

Ocean marine insurance offers both named and open peril protection for cargo and ships as they are transported over sea. It provides coverage against the following types of perils:

- Fire
- Explosion
- Pilferage
- Damage from ship condensation
- Other cargo contact
- Perils of the sea (**unusual wind or waves**; **stranding**) which occurs when the ship become immobilized due to **sinking, collision** and/or **lightning**
- Barratry, which occurs when the ship's crew willfully and illegally damages cargo
- Jettison

Jettison is known as **general average loss.** It is a term applied to any instance in which part of the cargo must be jettisoned to protect the remaining property. The cost of the cargo loss is shared proportionally by every property owner and the ship owner, no matter whose property was released. The term **particular average loss** applies to other types of partial property losses in which the damage is not shared by every property owner. Ocean marine insurance includes four categories: hull insurance, cargo insurance, freight insurance, and protection and indemnity (P&I) insurance.

Hull insurance covers physical damage to a ship or a fleet of ships moving over any body of water. The **running down clause** provides limited liability insurance when the insured's vessel is legally liable for damaging another vessel.

Cargo insurance insures goods being transported over water. It provides coverage on a trip or voyage basis (which covers a specific shipment) or an open cargo basis (which covers a specific period of time). The **warehouse to warehouse clause** extends coverage to protect the shipment as it stays at both its point of origin and its destination.

Freight insurance covers loss of shipping costs when cargo is destroyed or damaged during transit. It can stand as a separate policy, or it can be attached to hull insurance or cargo insurance. Freight insurance is purchased by either the cargo owner or the shipper, depending on prepayment requirements. If the cargo owner must prepay shipping costs, he is likely to purchase freight insurance as part of cargo insurance because he stands to lose if the cargo is lost. However, if the shipper does not require prepayment, he assumes the risk, and is likely to purchase freight insurance as part of hull insurance.

Protection and indemnity (P&I) insurance covers liability associated with the following marine-related accidents: injuries sustained by sailors in the course of their job duties; injuries sustained by longshoremen, harbor workers, and stevedores; cargo damaged due to negligence; collision damage to other property; non-collision damage to other property.

Implied warranties are part of ocean marine insurance, and help meet safety and public standards. Although implied warranties are not a written part of the policy, they are as valid as any other policy condition, and a failure to fulfill them can result in contract voidance. There are several implied warranties:

- **Seaworthiness** – This requires that the vessel is fit, properly loaded, and operated by a competent crew. Insurers will not cover losses if the ship is overloaded or stowing contraband.
- **Conditions of cargo** –This requires that cargo is sound, warranted, and packed correctly.
- **Legality** – This requires that the trip's enterprise is lawful.
- **No deviation in voyage** – This requires that the ship follow a predetermined route without destination changes or untoward delays.

According to the nationwide definition, there are six categories of risk eligible for marine insurance:

- Imports – covered by ocean marine insurance
- Exports – covered by ocean marine insurance
- Personal property floater risks – covered by personal inland marine insurance
- **Domestic shipments** – covered by **commercial inland marine insurance**, usually via transportation forms that apply specifically to transported property
- **Instrumentalities of transportation or communications** – covered by **commercial inland marine insurance**, usually via forms that apply to transportation or communication property (bridges, television antennas, etc.)
- **Commercial property floater risks** – covered by **commercial inland marine insurance** via bailee's customer forms, equipment forms, business floaters, and dealer's policies

In most cases, commercial inland marine coverage is limited to portable properties. Stationary properties, such as real estate, fixtures, and merchandise are not covered.

INLAND MARINE INSURANCE

Inland marine insurance covers property as it is being transported over land. It provides the same coverages found on ocean marine insurance, as well as several additional coverages. Inland marine policy forms fall under two classifications: non-filed and filed. **Non-filed classes** cover many different types of property, and each type uses a unique policy form. **Filed classes** apply to a far more specific range of property types. There are 12 different coverage forms. They are: mail, theatrical property, film, surgical and medical equipment, camera and musical instrument dealers, equipment dealers, commercial articles, accounts receivable, valuable papers/records, jewelers block, signs, and floor plan. Only filed classes of forms can be included in the commercial inland marine coverage part of the **ISO commercial package policy**, which consists of the following forms:

- Common policy declarations
- Common policy conditions
- Commercial inland marine declarations

- Commercial inland marine conditions
- At least one of the 12 coverage forms for filed classes

According to the **insured's duties in the event of a loss** condition, if a loss occurs, the insured must do the following:

- Alert the police when a law has been broken.
- Notify the insurer of the loss in a timely manner.
- Provide the insurer with a description of the damaged property and the time, place, and location of the loss.
- Protect the property against further damage and record any expenses incurred due to the loss.
- Assume no liability or obligation unless the insurer gives consent.
- Allow the insurer to inspect the damaged property and pertinent records.
- Provide sworn testimony when necessary.
- Submit a signed and sworn statement of loss to the insurer within 60 days from the date it is requested.
- Provide the insurer with any requested legal documents or notices in a timely manner.
- Assist investigatory as they work to settle the claim.

The **other insurance condition** mandates that, if the insured has a commercial inland policy and another policy written on the same basis, the commercial inland form provides reimbursement on a pro rata basis. However, if the two policies are covering the same property, but are not written on the same basis, the commercial inland form provides reimbursement in excess of the other insurance.

According to the **reinstatement of limit after a loss condition**, payment of a claim cannot reduce the limit of insurance. Such a reduction can only occur when a scheduled item is completely lost. In this case, the insured is repaid any unearned premiums.

PERSONAL INLAND MARINE INSURANCE

Personal inland marine insurance covers personal property as it is transported over water. These policies, commonly known as **floaters**, consist of a basic form. It explains all standard conditions, and is attached to one of the following personal inland marine forms: personal article form, personal property form, or personal effects form. These policies offer open peril protection with the following exclusions:

- Inherence vice, which is a defect inherent in the property
- Regular deterioration
- Expected wear and tear
- Insects
- Vermin
- Nuclear-related risks
- War

Personal inland marine insurance includes a **pair or set condition**, and can use one of the following reimbursement methods: repair/replace/restore the damaged set, or reimburse the difference between the actual cash value of the full set and the actual cash value of the undamaged portion of the set.

NATIONAL FLOOD INSURANCE PROGRAM

Communities acquire flood insurance through the **National Flood Insurance Program**, or **NFIP**, which is a federally subsidized program managed by the Federal Insurance Administration, or FIA. Although federal law requires flood-prone communities to apply to the NFIP, many apply voluntarily. When acquiring insurance, communities must complete and submit an NFIP application and pay the gross policy premium in full. Then, they must wait 30 days from the application date before coverage takes effect. This waiting period is waived in the following situations:

- Any waiting period is negated if the insurance is purchased in conjunction with a loan.
- If existing insurance is covering property whose title is being transferred, the coverage takes effect on the day of title transference.
- For first-time participants in the program, coverage goes into effect at 12:01AM on the day after the community mails the application and premium payment.
- Changes made to an existing policy go into effect at 12:01AM on the fifth day after the changes and the premium payment have been mailed.

FLOOD INSURANCE

Flood insurance covers virtually any walled or roofed building that is fixed to a permanent, above ground location. Coverage is available for both the building and its contents (i.e. personal property). Under the NFIP (National Flood Insurance Program), communities receive two types of flood insurance programs—emergency and regular. **Emergency coverage** applies as soon as the community submits the application, and provides limited coverage for buildings and their contents on a subsidized basis. This coverage carries a standard deductible of $1,000, and offers maximum coverage limits of $35,000 for buildings and $10,000 for building contents. **Regular coverage** applies after the NFIP receives the application and determines rates for the community. It carries a standard deductible of $500, and offers maximum coverage limits of $250,000 for buildings and $100,000 for building contents.

Flood insurance covers losses resulting from the following: inland or tidal water overflow, mudslides and/or mudflows, rapid water runoff or accumulation, and erosion or land collapse caused by flooding. The NFIP insures property against any direct loss caused by the above types of damage. When personal property is moved to a different location in order to protect it from flood damage, it is covered for a maximum of 45 days at the new location if it is being protected from weather damage. The NFIP does not cover the following types of property:

- Accounts, manuscripts, deeds, and most types of currency or financial notes
- Lawns (trees, shrubs, etc.), crops, and livestock
- Motor vehicles, self-propelled vehicles, and aircraft
- New buildings constructed over or in water
- Outdoor pools, fences, barrier walls, and open structures over waters, such as docks, wharves, etc.
- Wells, septic tanks, and other underground structures
- Containment structures like gas and liquid tanks

Replacement cost is the standard reimbursement method for building damage, and will be paid in full as long as the building is insured for 80% of its replacement value or the insured has purchased the maximum allowable coverage limit on the flood policy.

Actual cash value is the reimbursement method if the insured fails to meet the 80% criteria for replacement cost.

Debris removal is provided as long as the policy limit is large enough to cover both the expense amount and the direct loss amount.

The **Write Your Own program** is a Federal Insurance Administration (FIA) program that enables private insurers to sell NFIP insurance. The FIA determines coverage conditions, eligibility requirements, and rates, while the insurer handles premiums and loss reimbursements. The insurer must return to the government any premium surpluses (the amount by which premiums collected exceeds the loss reimbursement amount). However, the FIA covers any premium deficit. A deficit occurs when the premiums collected are insufficient to cover all losses.

PERSONAL ARTICLE FORMS

The **personal article form**, which is a type of inland marine insurance, provides coverage for the following property categories: silverware, golf equipment, stamps, coins, fine arts, jewelry, cameras, furs, and musical instruments. When newly acquired property falls under one of the last five categories, it is automatically covered under the policy with the following stipulations: All newly acquired property other than fine art is covered for 30 days at either 25% of the insurance limit or $10,000, whichever is less. Newly acquired fine art is covered for 90 days at 25% of the insurance limit. After the 30- or 90-days elapse, the insured must notify the company of the new property, or the coverage expires. Although personal article forms require an appraisal immediately after the policy is issued, they do not pay back losses on a valued basis. Instead, losses are reimbursed at actual cash value, repair cost, replacement cost, or an amount identified in the policy—whichever value is smallest.

PERSONAL PROPERTY FORM AND THE PERSONAL EFFECTS FORM

The **personal property form**, a type of inland marine insurance, offers open peril protection for 13 personal property categories, which encompass virtually every type of personal property found in the average home. Each category has a separate limit, and the insured should schedule valuable property separately.

The **personal effects form**, another type of inland marine insurance, insures personal property when the insured and his or her family are traveling. It provides open peril protection for cameras, clothing, souvenirs, and other types of property that tourists often carry. This form excludes the following types of property from coverage: passports, tickets, currency, valuable papers, contact lenses, sales samples, artificial limbs, and property in storage or on the insured's premises. Personal effect coverage is often acquired on a short-term basis.

PERSONAL WATERCRAFT INSURANCE AND OUTBOARD MOTOR AND BOAT INSURANCE

Personal watercraft insurance is provided through boatowner's/watercraft package policies, personal yacht policies, and other types of ocean marine forms and inland marine forms. In most cases, this insurance only covers watercraft used for personal enjoyment. Coverage does not apply when the craft is being used for transportation in exchange for a fee, being chartered out, or racing in an official contest.

Outboard motor and boat insurance, which is commonly written into inland marine policies, covers physical damage to the insured's watercraft, as well as collision damage to other watercraft. These policies normally reimburse damage to motors, motor boats, trailers, and equipment at actual cash value.

Boatowner's/watercraft package policies offer open peril protection for boats of a certain maximum length. Coverage includes property, liability, and medical up to a maximum dollar limit specified in the policy. Reimbursement is made at actual cash value. An insured may require additional liability coverage under a separate policy, such as a homeowner's policy.

PERSONAL YACHT POLICIES

Personal yacht policies provide open peril coverage for inboard boats, large pleasure boats, self-powered sailboats, and high value smaller boats in good condition. Yacht policies are ocean marine forms offering the following types of property and liability coverage:

- Hull insurance, which reimburses replacement cost for partial losses and valued cost for total losses
- Boat trailer insurance, which reimburses at actual cash value
- Medical payments insurance
- Protection and indemnity (P&I) insurance, which provides liability coverage for bodily injury and property damage
- Federal longshore and harbor worker's compensation insurance

In most cases, small boats can only receive hull insurance on a property coverage basis. Insureds should seek additional liability coverage under homeowner's policies.

A **collision clause**, which is part of hull insurance, provides liability coverage when the insured is responsible for collision damage to another watercraft. This coverage reimburses an amount equal to the property coverage on the hull, and must be exhausted before the P&I collision coverage can be used.

According to the **water-skiing clause**, any person who is skiing or being towed off the boat is not covered until they return to the vessel or arrive safely on dry land.

Layup warranty covers yachts that are being stored in a safe berth. This coverage normally applies during the winter months when the insured is not using the vessel, and may offer a premium repayment for the insured's risk reduction efforts.

The **navigational limits** clause is included on every yacht policy, and defines the operational area of the yacht. Unless the insurer agrees otherwise, losses are not covered if they occur beyond this area.

PERSONAL UMBRELLA INSURANCE

Personal umbrella insurance provides greater liability protection than personal line policies, with coverage limits between $1 million and $5 million. However, it only offers coverage on top of an existing policy. Therefore, a person must inform an insurer of his existing liability coverage before he can acquire a personal umbrella policy. For example, assume an individual purchases a homeowner's policy with a $200,000 liability limit and an umbrella policy with a $3 million limit. Before he can collect any amount from the umbrella policy, a liability loss must exceed the homeowner's policy limit, in this case $200,000. If the homeowner's policy lapsed before the loss occurred, the insured would be forced to pay $200,000 in damages before the umbrella policy would pay anything. Personal umbrella insurance may protect against losses that the underlying policy excludes. Covering such losses involves a **retention limit**, which is the loss amount the insured must pay before coverage applies. These limits, ranging from $250 to $10,000, are chosen by the insured.

CORPORATE INSURANCE PROVIDERS

Stock companies and mutual companies are the most common types of insurance providers. Stock companies operate by using money generated from the sale of stock. Stockholders are not required to purchase insurance from their company, and can acquire insurance from any provider without affecting their ownership rights or the dividends they receive.

Mutual companies are owned by the policyholders themselves who vote on management decisions and receive dividends like stockholders. Mutual companies take one of two possible forms:

- **Advance premium** – This is the most common form because it charges non-assessable premiums, meaning policyholders are never assessed any fees other than their premium payments, regardless of whether or not a loss occurs.
- **Assessment** – This is much less common because policyholders may be charged a pro rata share to cover losses. Assessment companies have highly variable costs of coverage, and primarily offer fire and windstorm protection for properties in rural areas.

INSURANCE PROVIDERS

Fraternal benefit societies are incorporated, but offer no stock and do not operate for profit. In most cases, they offer only health and life insurance. They typically function under a lodge system, whereby they only offer coverage and benefits to members of the society. Fraternals often use **open contracts**, which incorporate the society's charters, bylaws, and any amendments to the charter. Although the contract can change if the charter is amended, a fraternal can never take away benefits.

Lloyd's associations are not companies; rather, they are a group of people, or **syndicates**, who voluntarily pool their resources to insure contracts. A syndicate is personally responsible for the insurance amount that he or she drafts. Lloyd's associations are named for **Lloyd's of London**.

A **risk retention group** consists of multiple product manufacturers who want to insure themselves against product liability. These groups were established under the Liability Risk Retention Act of 1981, and include **self-insurance programs** and **captive insurance companies**. Risk retention groups are regulated in their states of origin, and require valid licensing in a minimum of one state in which they conduct business.

A **purchasing group**, which was also established under the Liability Risk Retention Act of 1981, is a group of businesses operating within the same industry or trade. These businesses purchase liability insurance collectively. Purchasing groups are regulated in their states of origin, but need not be licensed since they are only insurance purchasers. Both purchasing groups and risk retention groups are allowed to conduct business in multiple states.

A **reciprocal insurer**, also known as an exchange, is an unincorporated group of people who insure each other. The group shares insurance costs, as well as any losses incurred by its members. An **attorney-in-fact** is responsible for managing the reciprocal and all of its business.

Self-insured organizations and individuals have chosen not to acquire protection from an insurance provider and simply cover any losses with their own resources. Self-insured organizations and individuals tend to be quite wealthy.

Government insurance is provided by state or federal governments rather than private insurers. State governments often insure people who are too high of a risk for private insurers against

51

unemployment, worker injury, disability, medical malpractice, and property damage. The federal government may provide insurance against catastrophic loss (floods, weather, etc.) or **residual market insurance** to subsidize private carriers.

SYSTEMS BY WHICH INSURANCE PROVIDERS SELL INSURANCE

An **exclusive** (or **captive**) **agency system** is a system in which the insurance company contracts agents from independent agencies. The agents work on commission, and represent and sell insurance for only one contracting company.

A **direct writer system** is a system in which agents are actually employed by the insurance company, not a separate agency. The agents can work for commission, a salary, or a combination of the two.

Independent agency systems rely on **independent** or **nonexclusive agents**, who represent and sell insurance for more than one provider. The agency contracts independently with multiple providers and the agents work entirely on commission.

Direct response systems do not use agents. Instead, the provider uses mediums such as the Internet, the telephone, and mail to sell insurance directly to the client.

MAIL COVERAGE FORM

Mail coverage forms are part of the domestic shipment category of commercial inland marine insurance. They cover property loss on an open peril basis if the property is in the care or custody of a government postal service, and is being transported by a common carrier via registered mail, first class mail, express mail, or certified mail. Coverage lasts until the property reaches its location, and applies to stamps, money orders, checks, stock certificates, bonds, deposit certificates, and various other security certificates (money, food stamps, and unsold traveler's checks are not covered). Bullion, platinum, precious metals, watches, jewelry, and precious and semiprecious stones are covered only if they are transported by registered mail. Property loss is valued on an actual value basis, but cannot be less than the property's market value. The insured must report the value of the covered property every 30 days. If the property loss exceeds the limit of insurance, the reimbursement amount will equal the proportion the limit of insurance holds to the actual value.

THEATRICAL PROPERTY COVERAGE FORMS

Theatrical property coverage forms are part of the **equipment floater subcategory** of the commercial property floater risk category. They provide open peril protection for scenery, props, and costumes that a theatre group is using in a production specified under the policy's declarations section. The property can be owned by the insured or in his care or custody. These forms insure against collapse, provided it was caused by a covered peril. The following perils are excluded from coverage:

- Standard perils excluded on other commercial inland marine forms
- Theft when a vehicle is left unlocked or unattended
- Shortage discovered during inventory taking
- Unexplained disappearances

Additionally, these forms do not cover all types of property, such as buildings (including improvements and betterments), vehicles, animals, contraband, jewelry, currency, money, deeds, accounts, bills, admission tickets, and securities.

52

FILM COVERAGE FORM

Film coverage forms are part of the **equipment floater subcategory** of the commercial property floater risk category. They insure exposed motion picture film, soundtracks, videotapes, and magnetic tapes on an open peril basis. The property must be part of a production identified in the declarations section, and must be owned by the insured or under his care. Film coverage forms also provide collapse coverage, but do not cover positive prints or films, library stock, cutouts, or unused footage. The following perils are excluded from coverage:

- Standard perils excluded on other commercial inland marine forms
- Light exposure to negative film
- Temperature changes, atmospherically induced wetness, and deterioration
- Erasure or damage to electronic records and videotapes caused by electric or magnetic sources other than lightning
- Developing chemicals
- Film cutting, developing, printing, etc.

The reimbursement amount is determined by adding the cost of reproducing the damaged property to any value the undamaged portions of the production may have lost. The coverage area is limited to the U.S., U.S. territories, Canada, and any area within 50 miles of these locations.

COMMERCIAL ARTICLES COVERAGE FORMS AND SIGNS COVERAGE FORMS

Commercial articles coverage forms are part of the **equipment floater subcategory** of the commercial property floater risk category. They provide worldwide open peril protection for commercial cameras, musical instruments, and similar commercial property that is owned by the insured or in his care or custody. When the insured acquires new property that is included under the policy form, it receives limited coverage for 30 days. Afterwards, the insured must report it to the insurer or lose coverage.

Signs coverage forms are part of the **business floater subcategory** of the commercial property floater risk category. They provide open peril coverage for neon, fluorescent, automatic, and mechanical electric signs or lights that are owned by the insured's business or in its care. They do not cover breakage during transport or installation. Both forms (commercial articles and signs) provide standard collapse coverage and include the standard inland marine insurance exclusions.

ACCOUNTS RECEIVABLE COVERAGE FORMS

Accounts receivable coverage forms are part of the **business floater subcategory** of the commercial property floater risk category. When the company's accounts receivable records are damaged and the insured is unable to collect payments from his customers, these forms reimburse the lost customer payments, as well as any extra collection expenses that the insured incurs when he must take out a loan to maintain business operations while the damage is being repaired. Only account records stored on the premises are covered, and they must be stored in containers identified in the declarations section if they are not being used or the business is closed. These forms also cover collapse and removal, provided the records are being removed to protect them from a covered peril and the insured provides written notification within 10 days of the removal.

Accounts receivable coverage forms exclude the following losses from coverage:

- Changing, destroying, or concealing coverage forms as a means of covering up illegal or wrongful behavior
- Errors in bookkeeping, accounting, or billing

- Erasure of electronic data or recordings due to the following: electrical or magnetic interference, errors in programming, loss of power or power surge occurring 100 feet from the insured premises, any other problem occurring 100 feet from the insured premises, and flawed installation or repair of data processing equipment

These forms use a special reimbursement method when the insured cannot determine an accurate accounts receivable amount following a loss. The insurer takes an average monthly amount for accounts receivable from the previous 12 months, adjusts this average for any applicable variances and fluctuations, and then subtracts the following amounts: accounts that have sustained no loss, unearned interests, service charges, accounts the insured is able to recover, and bad debts the insured cannot collect.

VALUABLE PAPERS AND RECORD COVERAGE FORMS

Valuable papers and records coverage forms are part of the **business floaters subcategory** of the commercial property floater risk category. They cover the costs of replacing lost deeds, books, manuscripts, films, maps, and drawings that are owned by the insured or in his care. Collapse coverage and removal coverage (up to $5,000) are also provided, as long as they are necessitated by a covered peril. These forms include all the standard inland marine exclusions, including the following: loss of electronic data due to erasure, electrical interference or disturbance, and copying and processing errors. Coverage only applies if the papers and records are stored in accordance with the requirements listed in the declarations section. Each covered item has an insurance limit that coincides with its value listed in the declarations section. After the loss is settled, the insured may be required to adjust the reimbursement amount if he recovers the property.

JEWELERS BLOCK COVERAGE FORMS

Jewelers block coverage forms are part of the **dealer's policy subcategory** of the commercial property floater risk category. Unlike most types of inland marine insurance, these forms cover property that is on the business premises rather than in transit. The following types of property are covered:

- Stock used in the insured's business, such as jewelry, precious metals, and precious and semiprecious stones
- Sold merchandise that is awaiting shipment on the insured premises
- Similar property of others in the insured's care when the property owners are not in the jewelry trade
- Similar property of others in the insured's care when the property owners are in the jewelry trade (This coverage will not exceed the insured's legal liability in the property)

Jewelers block coverage forms include collapse coverage as well as the following optional coverages: **show window coverage** (which insures against theft of stock that is being displayed in a window that has been broken) and **money coverage** (which provides theft coverage for money stored in safes and faults located at the insured location).

Jewelers block coverage forms exclude the following losses from coverage:

- Standard commercial inland marine insurance exclusions
- Water damage occurring at the insured's premises
- Property stolen from a vehicle when it is not occupied by the person whose sole job is to watch the vehicle
- Faulty packaging

- Damage to highly breakable items
- Inventory shortages
- Items whose disappearance cannot be explained
- Loss due to the insured, his employees, or his workers committing illegal or dishonest acts
- Property shortage discovered after a package has been shipped if all the packing seals are unbroken

Jewelers block coverage reimburses losses using whichever of the following options represents the lowest amount: actual cash value, replacement cost, restoration cost (of the property right before it was damaged), or the lowest value of the property as listed by inventory. Coverage will be suspended if the insured fails to maintain the property's protective safeguards during closing hours, or if he fails to perform physical inventory once every 12 months.

FLOOR PLAN COVERAGE FORMS

Floor plan coverage forms are part of the **dealer's policy subcategory** of the commercial property floater risk category. They cover **encumbered merchandise**, which is merchandise that a dealer purchases using money borrowed from a lender. This relationship is known as a floor plan arrangement. Floor plan coverage can apply to both the dealer's interests and the lender's interests. It also provides collapse coverage, and excludes the following losses from coverage:

- Water damage occurring at the insured's premises
- Bankruptcy, foreclosure, etc.
- Property damage resulting from open exposure to rain, sleet, snow, freezing, or hail
- Damage to breakable items and glass
- Electrical damage to covered property caused by artificial currents

According to the **transit coverage in the event of cancellation condition**, if property is in the process of being transported when the policy is cancelled, the policy will continue to cover the property until it reaches its destination.

Dual interest condition holds that all parties must abide by policy provisions. It also protects the interests of the lender (provided it has tried to fulfill its contractual requirements) when other parties fail to fulfill policy provisions.

Reporting basis condition states that policy premiums will be calculated on a monthly basis using **reports of value**, which the insured must file within 30 days of the end of the month. The insurer is only required to pay 90% of the limit of insurance if the insured has not filed a new report prior to the loss. Additionally, the insurer is only required to cover the previous reported value if a new report of value is not filed by the deadline.

CAMERA AND MUSICAL INSTRUMENT DEALERS COVERAGE FORMS

Camera and musical instrument dealer's coverage forms are part of the **dealer's policy subcategory** of the commercial property floater risk category. They provide open peril coverage for the insured's stock in trade (in this case, cameras and musical instruments), as well as cameras and musical instruments owned by others but in the insured's possession or care. These forms provide theft and collapse coverage, and require the insured to maintain protective safeguards and inventory lists. Losses are reimbursed at:

- Actual cash value, replacement cost, or restoration value when the loss involves unsold property, whichever represents the lowest amount.
- Actual cash value or the insured's liability amount when the loss involves the property of others, whichever represents the lower amount.
- Net selling price minus allowances and discounts when the loss involves sold property that has not yet been delivered.

 Negatives and prints are valued at the cost of unexposed film plus labor and materials.

Camera and musical instrument dealer's coverage forms exclude the following losses from coverage:

- Standard inland marine insurance exclusions
- Earthquake damage occurring at the insured's premises
- Water damage occurring at the insured's premises
- Light exposure
- Marring or scratching
- Disappearances when there is no explanation
- Inventory shortages
- Electrical damage resulting from artificial current
- Breakage of glass items unless the item is a lens
- Theft from a car when it is left unlocked and unoccupied and exhibits no indication of forced entry

Additionally, these forms do not cover the following items: sold property after it has been delivered to customers; fixtures, office supplies, improvements, betterments, furniture, machinery, etc.; money, accounts, and other types of securities; property in the process of being mailed.

EQUIPMENT DEALERS COVERAGE FORMS

Equipment dealer's coverage forms are part of the **dealer's policy subcategory** of the commercial property floater risk category. They provide open peril coverage for mobile agricultural equipment and construction equipment that is part of the insured's stock-in-trade, or is owned by someone else but in the insured's care. These forms provide coverage for theft, attempted theft, and collapse. Losses are reimbursed at:

- Actual cash value, replacement cost, or restoration value when the loss involves unsold property, whichever represents the lowest amount.
- Actual cash value or the insured's liability amount when the loss involves the property of others, whichever represents the lower amount.
- Net selling price minus allowances and discounts when the loss involves sold property that has not yet been delivered.

These forms exclude the following losses from coverage:

- Standard inland marine insurance exclusions
- Water damage occurring at the insured's premises
- Inventory shortages

- Disappearances when there is no explanation
- Electrical damage from artificial current

Pollutant clean up and removal coverage applies when a covered peril has caused pollutant to discharge onto the insured's property. It provides $10,000 per 12-month period to cover the cost of extracting and removing pollutants.

Debris removal coverage covers the cost of removing debris from the insured's property when the debris is caused by a covered loss. The reimbursement limit equals 25% of the amount of the direct physical loss plus the deductible. This limit can be increased by $5,000 in the following situations: the total cost of debris removal and direct loss is greater than the limit of insurance, or the cost of debris removal is greater than the 25% limit.

For both coverages (debris removal and pollutant clean-up) to apply, the insured must submit an expense report within 180 days of the loss or the end of the policy period, whichever is earlier.

Jewelers block coverage does not apply if the property:

- Has been sold as part of a deferred sales payment agreement following its departure from the insured's premises.
- Is on display in showcases at locations other than the insured's premises.
- Is on display at exhibitions produced or funded by trade associations or public authorities.
- Is being worn by the insured, his family members, or his employees.
- Is being shipped by mail (except registered mail) or most other types of carriers.

Equipment dealer's coverage does not apply to the following types of property: automobiles, watercraft, and aircraft; money and other securities; leased, rented or sold property; office supplies, fixtures, furniture, machinery, improvements, patterns, etc.; property of others listed in the declarations section; property as it is being manufactured.

PHYSICIANS AND SURGEONS EQUIPMENT COVERAGE FORM

Physician's and surgeon's equipment coverage forms are part of the **equipment floater subcategory** of the commercial property floater risk category. They cover the following items on an open peril basis:

- Medical and dental instruments used by the insured (even if they are owned by others), regardless of whether they are kept on or off the premises
- Office fixtures and furniture
- Improvements and betterments

These forms also protect against theft, attempted theft, and collapse caused by covered perils. If any protective safeguards (security systems, sprinkler systems, etc.) were in place at the beginning of the coverage period, they must be maintained by the insured. Otherwise, the insurer suspends coverage until they are in working condition.

Physicians and surgeon's equipment coverage forms exclude the following perils from coverage:

- Light exposure, marring, or scratching
- Damage sustained when the insured, his employees, or anyone else with an interest in the property commits a criminal or dishonest act

57

- Nuclear dangers/Act of government
- Act of war or military
- Loss of use, loss of market, delay, consequential losses, etc.
- Electrical damage caused by artificial currents
- Fraudulence or trickery that caused the insured to voluntarily give up property
- Weather
- Loss caused by insects, rodents, and vermin
- Wetness, heat, cold, rust, and other forms of corrosion
- Mechanical breakdown
- Insured's neglect to protect property during and after a loss
- Natural wear, tear, and deterioration
- Inherent defects
- Unauthorized transference of property to another person
- Actions or decisions of the insured, or failures thereof
- Poor workmanship, planning, zoning, construction, maintenance, etc.

NONFILED INLAND MARINE FORMS THAT FALL UNDER THE DOMESTIC SHIPMENT CATEGORY

Parcel post policy provides coverage similar to the filed mail coverage form.

Annual transit policy provides named (fires, windstorm, theft, and collision) or open peril coverage for goods as they are being transported. This coverage is available to both the shipper and receiver, and applies to all shipments made over a one-year period.

Trip transit policy provides the same coverage as the annual transit policy, but only covers a single shipment.

Motor truck cargo policy, also known as the **motor truck cargo—truckers form**, provides liability coverage for carriers (not shippers) against damage to goods, provided the goods are being carried in a truck and the damage was not due to an act of God or negligence of the shipper.

Owner's goods on owner's truck policy, also known as the **motor truck cargo—shippers form**, is intended for shippers who carry their own goods. It covers against direct loss.

Motor truck cargo—combination form provides both liability and direct loss coverage.

BAILEE CUSTOMER POLICY

Bailee customer policies are a subcategory of the commercial property floater risk category, and include only non-filed classes of inland marine insurance forms. The **bailee's customer policy** provides liability coverage for bailees. When a bailee is in possession of a customer's property, and that property is damaged or destroyed by a covered peril, the policy reimburses the bailee so he may repay his customer. Different versions of the bailee's customer policy are available for different types of businesses. One such type is the **cleaners, dyers, and laundries policy**, which provides **confusion of goods coverage**. This coverage applies when the bailee (in this case the owner of the laundry service) suffers damage from a loss and is subsequently unable to differentiate between the garments of individual customers that are under his care.

CONTRACT EQUIPMENT FLOATER

The **contractor's equipment floater** is a non-filed form under the equipment floater subcategory of inland marine insurance. It provides named or open peril coverage for any tools, machinery, and

58

equipment that are owned by the insured or in his care. Coverage only applies when the property is being stored temporarily, being used on the job site, or being transited between locations. The dealer's policy subcategory offers non-filed forms for dealers of antiques, art, stamps, and coins. Coverage is provided on an open peril or a named peril basis and, depending on policy conditions, can apply to property that is on the premises, off the premises, or being transported. The **installation policy** covers property such as machinery, equipment, supplies, and building materials as they are in the process of being built, tested, installed, repaired, or renovated. Coverage only applies if the property is being used or transported in conjunction with the above tasks. Owners, sellers, and contractors can all obtain installation policies. The **electronic data processing equipment floater** covers computer hardware, software, and data on an open peril basis. The property can be owned by the insured or in his care, and can be in transit. Standard coverages include business interruption and extra expenses, while optional coverages include breakdown, which protects against mechanical breakdown, temperature fluctuations, and electrical damage.

FARM INSURANCE

Farm insurance provides personal and business coverage for farm businesses and homes, and can be acquired as a mono-line policy or as an inclusion in a commercial package policy. There are several types of **farm property coverage forms**, which offer the following:

- **Coverage A**—dwellings
- **Coverage B**—other private structures appurtenant to dwellings
- **Coverage C**—household personal property
- **Coverage D**—loss of use

Crops, trees, plants, shrubs, and lawns are excluded from coverage unless the insured acquires extensions under coverages A, B, and C. **Farm liability coverage forms** provide the following:

- **Coverage H**—bodily injury and property damage liability
- **Coverage I**—personal and advertising injury liability
- **Coverage J**—medical payments

These coverages exclude losses resulting from pollutants, injuries to farm employees, vehicles that are not identified by the policy, aircraft spraying, products of the insured, and actions or failures of action by the insured.

The **farm property—causes of loss form** identifies the perils against which farm property is insured, and provides three types of coverage: basic, broad, and special. The insured selects the type of coverage he needs. The **covered cause of loss—basic section** covers the standard perils found in other basic forms, including collisions that either kill covered livestock or damage covered farm machinery and personal farm property. The **covered cause of loss—broad section** includes the standard additional perils, including the following unique farm risks:

- Dog or wild animal attacks on covered livestock
- Covered livestock electrocution
- Covered livestock drowning
- Shooting covered livestock accidentally
- Loading/unloading accidents

The **covered cause of loss—special section** covers property on an open peril basis with the standard exclusions.

Property Insurance Terms and Related Concepts

DUTIES OF AN INSURANCE AGENT

An **insurance agent** represents the insurance provider to their clients and potential customers, and has several duties:

- **Selling insurance** – This generates commissions for the agent and revenue for the organization.
- **Countersigning** – This authenticates the contract. Agents must review and sign each new policy.
- **Providing quotations** – This informs potential clients of the premiums on a proposed contract. The agent is also responsible for acquiring information on clients, determining their needs, recommending coverage types, and assisting them in completing applications.
- **Field underwriting** – This involves determining the risk level of a particular business by using a set of established criteria.
- **Service needs** – This refers to any assistance the insured may require after the policy has been signed. Agents must help the insured with any policy changes, name changes, or claim filing. Agents should keep current records of these changes. They should reassess the sufficiency of the client's coverage on an annual basis.

INSURANCE PROFESSIONALS OTHER THAN AGENTS

Consultants charge a fee in exchange for insurance advice, such as explaining which policies are the most beneficial.

Solicitors have many of the same duties that agents have. They can represent the company, sell insurance, and receive premiums. However, they do not issue or countersign policies. Solicitors may work for agents.

Brokers are employed by the party seeking insurance. They represent the insured, and may speak with several different insurance companies in order to find the best offer. Brokers cannot bind or legally represent an insurance provider.

Excess or **surplus lines agents** sell **surplus lines of insurance**, which cover unique or high-risk situations. Very old homes, professional athletes looking to insure their bodies, tuition refunds, and medical malpractice are some examples of things that might be covered by surplus lines of insurance. These agents can handle surplus lines even in states where such insurance is not authorized.

Producers include all sellers of insurance, which includes agents and all of the professionals described above.

AGENCY RELATIONSHIP

Agency relationships are present wherever a principal (such as an insurance company) has empowered agents to act on its behalf. Insurance companies generally grant their agents the power to write contracts and receive payments. Because agents represent principals, any information presented to an insurance agent is simultaneously presented to the insurance company.

To better their reputation and increase their desirability, many agents earn professional accreditations and designations, such as **accredited advisor in insurance** (AAI), **chartered-property casualty underwriter** (CPCU), and **associate in person insurance** (API). These designations are offered by the **Insurance Institute of America** and the **American Institute for Chartered Property Casualty Underwriters**. Many states mandate that agents undergo continuous education to improve their skills and keep up with the latest knowledge, trends, and developments.

PROPERTY INSURANCE AND CASUALTY INSURANCE

Insurance providers are often classified according to the insurance line (or type) they write. One such line is **property insurance**, which covers damage to physical property and any income it produces. Another line is **casualty insurance**, which provides non-property coverage, such as liability, workers' compensation, crime, fidelity, and surety.

An insurance provider can be further classified as either **mono-line**, meaning it handles only one line of insurance, or **multi-line**, meaning it handles multiple lines. Lines can also be categorized as personal or commercial. **Personal lines** include property and casualty policies intended for persons and families. **Commercial lines** protect businesses. By analyzing statistical data on each line and gathering premium information, companies can determine the most profitable and least profitable insurance types.

PERIL AND HAZARD

Perils are the actual events that create loss, such as adverse weather, natural disasters, theft, industrial accidents, and fires. A peril is different from a risk in that a risk is the likelihood that a particular loss will occur.

Hazards are situations that increase the likelihood of loss. For instance, the presence of flammable construction material in a building increases the chance of fire damage. Therefore, the flammable construction material represents a hazard. There are three types of hazards:

- **Physical hazard** – This applies to the usage, occupancy, and state of the actual property. Flammable construction material is a type of physical hazard.
- **Moral hazard** – This describes a person's inclination for dishonest or illegal behavior. For example, people may damage their own property or mislead the insurance company in the hopes of getting money.
- **Morale hazard** – This applies to losses resulting from the careless or irresponsible behavior of a person.

DIRECT LOSS AND INDIRECT LOSS

The insuring agreements section specifies the type of loss (direct or indirect) covered by a property insurance policy. **Direct loss** is the result of physical damage, loss, or destruction to property, and can be caused by theft, fire, weather, and other similar perils. **Indirect loss**, also known as **consequential loss**, includes any financial hardships incurred as a byproduct of the direct loss. For instance, when a car is stolen, a person not only loses the value of his car, but may also incur additional expenses if he is forced to rent a car. The cost of automobile rental is an example of indirect loss. Another example would be the cost of renting a hotel room when a home is destroyed. Policies can extend their coverage to include indirect costs. In some instances, indirect coverage is a basic component of the policy.

CALCULATING THE REIMBURSEMENT VALUE OF A PROPERTY INSURANCE POLICY

When a loss occurs, the insurance provider calculates a reimbursement value using one of the following methods:

- **Actual cash value (ACV)** – This is the replacement cost of the insured item, minus any depreciation. If depreciation is not taken into account, the insured will actually gain money, thereby breaking the principle of indemnity.
- **Repair cost** – This is the amount necessary to repair any damage to the insured item.
- **Replacement cost** – This is the amount necessary to replace the item without accounting for depreciation. Full replacement costs are not usually awarded unless the insured meets certain criteria.
- **Functional replacement cost** – This is the amount necessary to repair or replace the item with materials that are less expensive but functionally the same.
- **Market value** – This is the current market worth of the item, which can increase and decrease over time.

Typically, the option that represents the lowest value is the one that will be used.

VALUATION AND COINSURANCE CONDITION

The **valuation condition** dictates that most losses will be reimbursed at actual cash value, unless the loss is $2,500 or less and the insured has met the coinsurance condition. In this case, the insurer reimburses the repair/replacement cost of the building without deducting depreciation. Valuation is also affected by the following factors: net selling price of its stock; cost of glass (valued at either replacement cost of glazing material if such material is required by law, or replacement cost of similar material if glazing material is not required by law); cost of blank media needed to replace lost or damaged valuable papers and records; cost of tenant improvements and betterments if they are paid for by the insured.

Coinsurance condition reduces the reimbursement amount if the insured has not met the coinsurance condition.

PROXIMATE CAUSE

Proximate cause is a natural and continuous action that results in damage or loss. An action cannot be considered a proximate cause unless:

- It occurs as a chain or sequence unbroken by independent factors.
- The loss would not have occurred if the action had been absent.

Assume, for instance, that a fire causes structural damage to a department store and the owner fails to exercise proper care in making repairs. The damage then leads to structural collapse that injures a shopper, who then sues the store and receives a settlement. The fire would be considered a proximate cause because it set off an unbroken chain of events that led to a loss (the settlement). Next, assume a thunderstorm occurs shortly after the structural damage. Water seeps into the store, which damages some of the merchandise. The fire is not the proximate cause of the damaged merchandise because the sequence of events was interrupted by an **intervening cause** (the thunderstorm) whose occurrence was not caused by the fire.

INSURANCE COMPANY DEPARTMENTS

Policy issue and administration reviews new applications after they have been approved by the underwriting department, and creates a policy form for the applicant. **Policy analysts**, also known as **screeners**, verify the accuracy and completeness of information included in the policy. **Raters** calculate the premium amount at which the policy should be assessed.

The **actuarial and statistical department** is filled with **actuaries** who establish separate rates for each insurance type by analyzing computer data and statistics gathered from other insurance providers.

The **investment department** invests company funds with the goal of not only earning enough money to pay claims and future obligations, but also generating a high rate of return for the company. Part of the investment must be easily liquefiable.

Miscellaneous support departments, which include general administration, assistance, training, management information systems, and maintenance, assist other departments in their operations.

The **claims department** is responsible for indemnifying (paying) insured parties after a loss occurs. This department includes **claims adjusters**, also known as **representatives**, who inspect the damage and determine if the loss is covered by the policy. They may even distribute payments. Depending on the company's size, claims adjusters can be employees or contract workers.

The **accounting department** issues the appropriate compensation (commissions, salaries, or a combination of the two) to agents, credits premiums to the correct accounts, and keeps up reserve accounts.

The **agency department** recruits, trains, selects, and directs agents. It is also responsible for tracking agent sales and matching agents with their most appropriate market.

The **marketing department** directs the marketing strategy of the company. It creates advertisements, and often works collaboratively with an advertising department.

The **audit department** handles policies for which premiums are not established until after the policy term has commenced. The audit department sets these premiums by examining the company's payroll, receipts, number of employees, and the accounting records of the insured.

The **loss control department**, sometimes called the **engineering department**, helps insured individuals reduce risk and avoid loss by recommending preventative measures.

The **legal department** ensures that the company is following all applicable laws and regulations. It interprets these laws, and handles any legal issues or court cases that arise in connection with the company. The legal department is also responsible for establishing the payout for policies.

The **reinsurance department** acquires insurance for the insurance provider. This process is known as reinsurance, and it protects the provider against losses resulting from unfavorable underwriting results.

POLICY LIMITS OF LIABILITY INSURANCE

A **policy limit** is the maximum amount an insurance policy will pay for any one loss, and is listed in the declarations section. Policy limits can be applied using a variety of methods:

- **Per occurrence** – The loss occurs in a particular place over a period of time. This method will cover losses caused by repeated exposure to a harmful condition over a long period of time.
- **Per accident** – The loss occurs in a much more specific place over a set period of time. This method is not used to cover losses caused by repeated and lengthy exposure to harmful conditions.
- **Per person** – There is a maximum reimbursement limit for any single person for a particular injury.

After a loss has been reimbursed, the full policy limit is restored and available for the next loss. However, the policy may also have an **aggregate limit**, which places a limit on the amount a policy can pay out per year. This limit is restored on an annual basis.

ADMITTED AND NONADMITTED COMPANIES AND DOMESTIC, FOREIGN, AND ALIEN COMPANIES

State insurance departments have certain responsibilities, such as determining whether or not insurance companies are conforming to state regulations. Conforming companies are known as **admitted** or **authorized insurers**, and are allowed to conduct business within the state. Non-conforming companies are known as **nonadmitted** or **unauthorized insurers**, and are only allowed to do business in very specific situations. Insurance departments also classify companies according to their state of incorporation. Under law, companies can only be incorporated in their home state, but can operate in any number of states or countries. **Domestic companies** are insurance providers that operate in their home states. **Foreign companies** are providers that operate in states other than their states of incorporation. If a company is operating in the U.S., but has been incorporated in another country, it is classified as an **alien company**.

REGULATIONS THAT INSURANCE PROVIDERS MUST FOLLOW

State insurance departments impose financial regulations on insurance companies. According to these regulations, companies must maintain certain capital and surplus requirements, distribute yearly financial statements, and disclose a certain level of financial data, depending on whether they are classified as a domestic, foreign, or alien company. By monitoring these disclosures, the insurance department can assess the financial health of a company in order to identify problems as early as possible, maintain solvency, and protect insured persons in the event of insolvency. Several states have **insurance guaranty associations**, which pay claims when an insurance provider suffers insolvency. States will also inspect insurance providers on an intermittent basis, assist the provider if it falls into financial trouble, and manage liquidations if the provider goes under. Independent organizations, such as S&P and Moody's, often rank insurance companies according to their financial strength. These rankings are based on factors such as investment performance and claims experience.

State insurance departments require that agents fulfill the following regulations:

- **Licensing** – Agents can only sell insurance in states in which they are properly licensed to do so. In order to receive a license, agents must pass a state insurance exam.
- **Maintain fiduciary relationships with clients** – Agents are required to receive and handle premiums from clients.

- **Avoid twisting** – Twisting is an illegal activity in which agents mislead clients into canceling their current policies and purchasing new ones. This is done solely to benefit the agent.
- **Avoid false advertising** – Agents cannot misrepresent any part of the policy or the company's financial information. All information must be accurate.
- **Avoid rebating** – Rebating is the practice of offering money, gifts, kickbacks, or any other benefit to coerce clients into purchasing insurance. (Rebating is actually legal in California and Florida)
- **Avoid unfair discrimination** – Agents must offer the same rate to all clients in identical situations, and cannot take bribes.

RATE-MAKING

Rate-making is when an insurance provider sets their own rates and presents them to the state. Rate-making is necessary in non-mandatory states, and rates are based on comprehensive operational, premium, financial, and loss statistics. Loss costs are the most important determinant of an insurance rate because they indicate the amount necessary to cover the company's expected losses. Insurance companies often seek membership in **service bureaus**, such as the Insurance Service Office (ISO) or the National Council on Compensation Insurance (NCCI). Service bureaus assist in gathering loss statistics and other relevant information. Service bureaus collect and analyze statistics from every membership company, and store them with their state insurance department. Companies can deviate from these rates within a certain range. When companies submit their rates to the state, they must identify where they obtained their loss data and any other determining factors, by either listing their service bureau or explaining that they collect their data independently.

MERIT RATING

Merit rating is the third method of calculating premiums, and is used when a risk has unusual or unique characteristics. In the merit rating method, an underwriter or agent determines a manual rating for the policy, and then adjusts it based on the unusual qualities of the risk. Common types of merit rating include experience rating, schedule rating, and retrospective rating. **Experience rating** examines the **loss experience** of the insured. In most cases, loss experience is the three-year difference between the premiums collected from the insured and the amount the insured has received in claims. If the insured's loss experience is worse than the average loss experience, the premium will be higher than the manual rate. If the insured's loss experience is better than the average loss experience, the premium will be lower than the manual rate. **Schedule rating** assesses a system of debits and credits according to the insured's characteristics. **Retrospective rating** considers any losses over the policy period.

POLICY PERIOD AND NONRENEWAL

The **policy period**, also known as the **policy term**, is the time between a policy's effective date and its expiration date. Essentially, it is the length of time that insurance is provided. Most policy terms are six months, one year, or three years, provided they are not cancelled. According to most state laws, if a policy is not renewed, its coverage ends at 12:01 AM (one minute after midnight) on the expiration date. Therefore, to maintain continuous coverage, the effective date of the new policy should fall on the same day as the expiration date of the old policy.

Nonrenewal options are normally given at the end of the policy period. Policy coverage is discontinued if the insured or the insurance provider chooses not to renew the policy after its expiration date. In most cases, insured individuals can exercise their nonrenewal options without having to fulfill any requirements. Insurance companies, however, may require a valid reason to decline renewal, and may need to provide notification.

AUTHORITY HELD BY INSURANCE AGENTS

Express authority includes any powers formally granted to the agent, such as the power to write specific insurance lines, countersign, issue policies, deliver policies, bind coverage, accept premiums, and settle claims. Because express authority is laid out in writing or verbally, the powers associated with this level are the most clearly defined.

Implied authority includes any powers that have not been formally granted, but are necessary for the agent to fulfill his duties. An example is the agent's ability to recommend and describe coverage options for the client.

Apparent authority is based on the assumptions of a "reasonable person" about the powers an agent should have. For instance, a reasonable person might assume that an agent represents the insurance company to the general public.

APPLICATION PROCESS FOR ACQUIRING INSURANCE AND BINDERS

Before insurance can be acquired, the person seeking insurance and the agent must complete an **application** and submit it to the insurance company. The application contains vital information about the client's risk level, and is the primary factor in the company's decision about whether or not to insure the client. Therefore, the agent must make sure that all information on the application is complete and accurate. If the agent neglects these duties, he may face lawsuits from both the agency and the client. After the application has been submitted, the agent may be empowered to issue a **binder**, which is a verbal or written agreement providing immediate insurance coverage to the client. Verbal binders must be transferred to a written document in a timely manner. Binders do not guarantee the application will be accepted, and can be cancelled via formal notice or when the new policy takes effect.

WAIVER AND ESTOPPEL

A **waiver** occurs whenever a person or organization intentionally gives up an established right. For instance, insurance companies may have the right to raise premiums, reduce benefits, and deny or revoke policies if certain contractual conditions or provisions are violated. In some cases, companies may deliberately relinquish (waive) these rights, even when they can exercise them. Not all rights can be waived, including facts and certain requirements for insurance, such as an insurable interest.

Estoppel protects innocent parties against damages resulting from coverage misrepresentation. In effect, if an insurance provider indicates (either deliberately or inadvertently) that a particular coverage is present, the provider cannot deny that coverage, even when it is not part of the policy.

FEDERAL REGULATION OF INSURANCE COMPANIES

Very little insurance regulation occurs at the federal level, but a few regulations and programs exist, such as the **Fair Credit Reporting Act**, the **National Flood Insurance Program**, and the **Federal Emergency Management Agency** (or **FEMA**). Federal regulations are especially concerned with **fraud and false statements**. Insurance personnel cannot deliberately misrepresent the value of property or securities in order to manipulate the actions of an insurance or regulatory agency. Additionally, insurance personnel cannot intentionally commit the following acts: embezzlement, abstraction, misappropriation, or purloining of insurance funds, premiums, or property. Anyone found guilty of violating federal insurance regulations may incur punishments ranging from heavy fines to up to 10 years in prison.

STATE REGULATION OF INSURANCE COMPANIES

Insurance companies are mainly regulated at the state level. Laws vary from state to state, but all states appoint a **commissioner**, also known as a **director** or **superintendent**, who oversees an **insurance department** responsible for regulating insurance activities. State insurance departments enforce laws and regulate the conduct of agents and companies, as well as the sale of various insurance types. When violations are reported, the department must conduct an investigation and levy penalties whenever necessary. Penalties include fines, the revocation or suspension of a company's license or its right to conduct business in a certain state, and even incarceration. The **National Association of Insurance Commissioners**, or **NAIC**, consists of commissioners from every state who meet periodically to coordinate activities, share knowledge, and make recommendations. There are no laws requiring states to implement NAIC recommendations, but most do.

SPECIFIC INSURANCE AND BLANKET INSURANCE

The declaration section describes the property being insured, and identifies whether the insurance is specific or blanket. **Specific insurance** establishes limits on the items being insured. Despite being designated as "specific," the policy does not have to list each item. However, every insured item must be part of the overall property. Consider, for instance, a homeowner's insurance policy. Even though the policy may not list any furniture or appliances, they are still covered. **Blanket insurance** can cover multiple properties at different locations. For example, a person who owns several buildings might purchase a blanket policy, thereby covering every building under the same policy. **Endorsements** are also part of the declaration section, and include any property covered by the policy. They are organized according to a form number. When agents and underwriters review endorsements, they should identify any restrictive endorsements (unexpected items) and any items that may have been accidentally omitted.

POLICY COVERAGES, ADDITIONAL COVERAGES, NAMED PERIL CONTRACTS, AND OPEN PERIL CONTRACTS

The following terms are included in the insuring agreements section of a property insurance policy:

- **Policy coverages** – These identify the different coverage types provided by the policy, as well as the property being insured.
- **Additional coverages** – These are items that may be covered under major limits, may have less liability coverage, or may be added if the applicant fulfills certain requirements. Additional coverages are also known as **other coverages**, **extended coverages**, or **coverage extensions**.
- **Named peril contracts** – These only protect against perils (such as fire, wind, flood, theft, etc.) that are specifically described within the insuring agreements section.
- **Open peril contracts** – These are also known as **all risk** contracts or **special coverage** contracts. They protect against all perils except those that are excluded by the insuring agreements section.

CONCURRENT CAUSATION

Concurrent causation describes a situation in which two perils occur either simultaneously or sequentially and create loss against the same policy. In the past, concurrent causation was a source of great confusion and ambiguity. If a named peril and an excluded peril occurred simultaneously and caused damage, the insured could demand indemnity under the named peril, while the insurance provider could deny indemnity under the excluded peril. Consider, for instance, a homeowner's policy that indemnifies against collapse but not earthquakes. Confusion arises if the collapse is the result of an earthquake. The homeowner is likely to seek damages under the collapse provision, and the insurance provider is likely to deny indemnity because the collapse was caused by an earthquake. As courts began ruling in favor of insureds, insurance companies were forced to use more precise wording, and newer policies began placing specific restrictions on named perils. For example, according to a newer policy, a collapse would only be covered if it were caused by a specific set of circumstances, such as fire or faulty building materials. In a newer policy, earthquakes would be explicitly excluded.

COINSURANCE CONDITION AND COINSURANCE PENALTY

According to the **coinsurance condition**, an insured will not be reimbursed to the policy's full limits unless he purchases a certain minimum amount of insurance. For example, if a property insurance policy has an 80% coinsurance condition, the insured must purchase a policy that covers at least 80% of the property's value. If the insured fails to meet the coinsurance condition, any loss he suffers must meet or exceed the amount he chose to insure. Otherwise, the insurance provider will only reimburse a percentage of the loss. Any unpaid loss is known as the **coinsurance penalty**, which is calculated as a proportion of the actual insured amount versus the required coinsurance amount. For some policies, coinsurance conditions are expressed as an actual dollar value rather than a percentage. These policies are known as **agreed value** or **stated amount** policies, and are used when the coinsurance penalty is difficult to predict.

The coinsurance penalty is calculated as a proportion of the actual insured amount versus the required coinsurance amount. It is applied when someone purchases a policy and fails to meet the coinsurance condition.

PAIR OR SET CONDITION

When a policy insures property that consists of two components, it often includes a **pair or set condition** as part of the loss settlement. Damage to one component will adversely affect the value of the other component. Therefore, according to the pair or set condition, if one component is damaged or destroyed, the insurance provider is not required to reimburse the value of the entire set. However, the insurer must consider how the damaged part affects the value of the set as a whole and adjust the reimbursement amount appropriately. Consider, for example, an antique desk and chair set worth $1,500 collectively, but only $500 if either part is lost. If the chair is destroyed, the insurance provider should pay out $1,000, which reimburses the loss in value.

SALVAGE CONDITION AND ABANDONMENT CONDITION

The **salvage condition** allows companies to purchase and take ownership of damaged property, and is one method of lowering claims expenses. If the policy includes a salvage condition, a company can pay an amount equaling the property's replacement cost, assume possession of the damaged property from the insured, and then resell it for the highest possible amount. If the insured wishes to stop the insurer from exercising this right, he must either reject the settlement offer or negotiate a lower one. Insurance companies are not required to salvage damaged property. They will only do so if they can make a profit, or if the cost of repair exceeds the value of the property. Salvaging is normally profitable when the loss is only partial or the damaged parts have scrap value.

The **abandonment condition** forbids the insured from abandoning his property and then demanding full reimbursement from the insurance company. Only the insurer can determine if the property should be repaired, replaced, or salvaged.

APPRAISAL CONDITION AND ARBITRATION CONDITION

The **appraisal condition** allows the insured and the insurer to resolve disputes over indemnification value. When neither side can agree on a reimbursement amount following a loss, each side can hire an independent appraiser using their own money. If the appraisers cannot agree on a value, they choose an umpire, essentially a third appraiser, to serve as an objective authority. A final indemnification value is reached when two of the three appraisers agree on an amount. The insured and the insurer split the cost of the umpire.

The **arbitration condition** is used to resolve several different kinds of disputes, not just those arising over indemnification value. Disputes may involve third party liability or two separate insurers.

OTHER INSURANCE CONDITION AND CONCURRENT AND NONCONCURRENT INSURANCE

The **other insurance condition** applies when there are multiple insurance policies covering the same property. It prevents the insured from receiving an excessive payout in the event of a loss, and explains how losses are reimbursed. One type of reimbursement is the **primary and excess** method, which is used when there are two different insurers. The first insurer, known as the **primary insurer**, pays out a certain portion of the loss. The second insurer, known as the **excess insurer**, agrees to pay any loss amount that exceeds the primary insurance amount. In the **pro rata liability** method, each policy covers a percentage of the loss as determined by its insurance limit. For instance, one insurer may pay 60%, while the other may pay 40%. When multiple policies cover the same property, they can be classified as either **concurrent**, meaning they protect against the same perils, or **nonconcurrent**, meaning they do not protect against the same perils. Nonconcurrent insurance poses several problems, and should be avoided in most cases.

LIBERALIZATION CONDITION, ASSIGNMENT CONDITION, AND NO BENEFIT TO BAILEE CONDITION

According to the **liberalization condition**, when insurance providers expand coverage on a policy or endorsement without increasing premium payments, the broadened coverage simultaneously applies to every comparable policy or endorsement. Because of this condition, insurers do not need to distribute new endorsements. Insureds are informed of the change at renewal time.

The **assignment condition** states that policies cannot be transferred to new holders unless the original holder provides written consent or dies. If the insured dies, his legal representative assumes all rights and duties under the policy through a process known as **transfer of rights or duties under this policy**.

According to the **no benefit to bailee condition**, a bailee (a person or group with temporary possession of another person's property) cannot collect a settlement from the insured's policy, even if the bailee is holding the insured's property when damage occurs.

MORTGAGE AND POLICY TERRITORY CONDITIONS, AND VACANCY AND UNOCCUPANCY PROVISIONS

The **mortgage condition** (also known as the **loss payable condition**) explains the duties and rights of any mortgagee who holds an insurable interest in the property. The mortgagee's duties may include filing a loss on behalf of the insured or making premium payments if the insured is unable to do so. These duties protect the mortgagee's policy interests, which may continue even if the insurer rescinds the insured's coverage at some point. In some cases, the insurer may have the right to pay off the mortgage and assume the mortgagee's interests.

According to the **policy territory condition** (also known as the **policy period condition**), a loss is not covered unless it occurs within the policy's territory, which usually consists of the U.S., Puerto Rico, and Canada.

Vacancy provisions apply when the insured area contains neither people nor property. **Unoccupancy provisions** apply when people are absent. These provisions allow the insurer to limit coverage, and are necessary because vacant or unoccupied property poses a greater risk.

GLOSSARY

Combined ratio is the sum total of the loss ratio and expense ratio. If the combined ratio exceeds 100%, the company has suffered a loss. If the combined ratio is less than 100%, the company has earned a profit.

Earned premium includes all corporate earnings related to providing insurance.

Expense ratio is the total underwriting expenses divided by the total written premiums, and is used to determine the cost of conducting business.

Incurred loss includes all corporate expenditures for handling or covering losses on claims.

Loss ratio is the incurred loss percentage divided by the earned premium, and is used to determine the annual performance of corporate operations.

Underwriting expenses include salaries, commissions, administrative costs, regulatory costs, and advertising.

Written premiums include all premium income, such as earned premiums, unearned premiums, renewals, policy endorsements, and new business.

Property Policy Provisions and Contract Law

EXCLUSIONS

The following types of exclusions are common in property insurance:

- **Nonaccidental losses** – These include damages resulting from mechanical breakdown, electrical breakdown, and wear caused by natural use. These losses are excluded from coverage due to their certain and unavoidable nature. Insurance can only cover uncertain events or risks.
- **Catastrophic losses** – These are devastating to the point that a company would go bankrupt trying to insure them. Examples include war, energy crises, and other similar catastrophes.
- **Property already covered by other insurance policies** – This type of property is excluded from coverage. If a person already has a homeowner's insurance policy, he cannot get additional property insurance to cover his home.

The following types of exclusions are common in property insurance:

- **Losses controllable by the insured** – These include scratches, breaks, chips, and any other damages that the insured can avoid simply by exercising caution. The policy excludes these losses in order to encourage the insured to act responsibly.
- **Extra-hazardous perils** – These include earthquakes and various unusual or unique causes of loss. In most cases, insureds do not want coverage on extra-hazardous perils because their likelihood of occurring is too small to justify the expense of the coverage. However, if an insured does require the coverage, he can acquire it by asking for an additional endorsement and paying additional premiums.

Liability insurance generally excludes the following losses from coverage:

- Bodily injury sustained by the insured
- Property damage when the insured owns the property
- Property damage when the insured has custody of the property
- Injuries and damages that the insured inflicts intentionally
- Losses already insured by worker compensation laws
- Losses already insured by Nuclear Energy Liability policies

Liability insurance normally includes the following conditions:

- **Duties after a loss** – The insured must send written notification to the insurer of all losses, demands, notices, and summonses, and must assist the insurer during the case. The insured cannot willingly reimburse another party for a loss or assume liability for a loss without first getting consent from the insurer.
- **Other insurance** – When multiple policies are covering the same loss, liability policies handle reimbursement on a **contribution by equal shares** basis. This means that each insurer reimburses an equal amount up to the smallest policy's limit until the loss has been paid off.

71

NAMED INSURED, FIRST NAMED INSURED, ADDITIONAL INSUREDS, AND POLICY LIMIT

The following terms are included within the declaration section of a property insurance policy:

- **Named insured** – This is the person or business that has been issued the policy.
- **First named insured** – This is the person or business on the policy with the most rights or duties. This designation is used when a policy insures more than one entity.
- **Additional insureds** – These are any other entities covered by the policy, and are usually listed in the declaration or endorsement section. It should be noted that a policy may cover items that are not listed in either the declaration or endorsement sections.
- **Policy limit** – This is the maximum amount a policy will indemnify (pay out) in the event of a loss, and is also known as a **limit of insurance**, **limit of coverage**, or **limit of liability**. This limit may involve a **value** (or **agreed**) **amount contract** if the coverage item is especially difficult to value. The insurer and the insured simply agree to pay out a certain amount if a loss occurs.

STANDARD CONDITIONS RELATED TO LOSS PROVISIONS

Every insurance policy contains a **conditions section**, which explains the responsibilities and rights of every party involved in the insurance contract. In most cases, the conditions section lists **loss provisions** that outline the duties of both insureds and insurance providers after a loss occurs. The insured's duties, known as **duties following loss**, normally include the following:

- Providing the insurance agent with a claim of loss in a timely manner
- Allowing the company to view the property
- Assisting the agent as he or she inspects the damage
- Filling out a **proof of loss** form, which inventories the damage
- Safeguarding the property against additional damage
- Being examined under oath

The insurance provider's duties are related to **valuation**, and are known as **how losses will be paid**. According to most policies, the insured is awarded one of the following: policy limits, insurable interest, actual cash value, replacement cost, or repair cost. Typically, the option that represents the lowest value is the one that will be awarded.

CAUSES OF LOSS FORMS

Causes of loss forms list the perils that are covered by commercial property insurance, and are divided into three types: basic, broad, and special.

The **cause of loss—broad form** insures against the following perils:

- All perils covered by the cause of loss—basic form
- Weight of ice, sleet, or snow
- Falling objects (only covers exterior damage unless the falling object created a hole in an outside wall)
- Water damage, such as seepage or leakage from a damaged water/steam system (also covers the cost of removing and replacing damaged water/steam systems)

The broad form provides **limited mold additional coverage** and **collapse additional coverage**. Collapse is only covered if it results from the following: glass breakage, weight of people and personal property, weight of rain on roof, hidden decay, defective building materials used for construction, remodeling, or renovation when the collapse occurs during construction, remodeling, or renovation, and hidden insect/vermin damage (unless the insured was aware of the damage prior to the collapse).

Cause of loss—basic form provides named peril coverage against the following perils: lightning, fire, explosion, windstorm or hail, aircraft or vehicles (except when owned or operated by the insured for his business), riot or civil commotion, vandalism, sinkhole collapse, volcanic eruption, sprinkler leakage, and smoke (except for agricultural smudging or industrial operations). The basic form excludes the following perils from coverage:

- Laws and ordinances (unless covered by an endorsement)
- Government action
- Fungus, bacteria, wet rot, and dry rot, unless they result from fire or lightning
- Nuclear dangers, Earth movement
- War/military activity
- Power or utility service failure originating beyond the insured premises
- Mechanical breakdown
- Steam boiler, pipe, engine, or turbine explosion
- Artificial electrical current, Water-related hazards
- Pipe rupture, except for automatic sprinklers
- Water or steam leakage caused by the breakage of water or steam systems

Limited coverage for fungus, wet rot, dry rot, and bacteria is an additional coverage available on the cause of loss—basic form. It covers damage resulting from fungus (which includes mold, mildew, spores, scents, mycotoxins, and fungal residue), and reimburses the following costs: removing mold and repairing direct physical property damage or loss caused by mold, removing and replacing portions of the building so one can gain access to the mold, and testing to determine the presence of mold after property repairs or replacements have been completed. The reimbursement amount cannot exceed $15,000 per year, no matter how many claims are filed. Coverage only applies if the damage occurs during the policy period and the mold is caused by a covered loss. Additionally, following the discovery of a mold occurrence, the insured must take reasonable steps to avoid further property damage.

The **collapse additional coverage** on the cause of loss—broad form covers the following outdoor properties when they sustain direct damage from a collapsed building:

- Radio/television antennas, satellite dishes, and their equipment
- Yard fixtures
- Awnings, gutters, and downspouts
- Piers, wharves, docks, etc.
- Fences
- Retaining walls
- Outdoor swimming pools
- Diving platforms
- Walks/roadways/paved surfaces

Even in the absence of building collapse, personal property collapse is covered, provided the property is inside a building, the collapse was cause by a named cause of loss, and the property is not one of the outdoor items listed above.

The **cause of loss—special form** provides open peril protection against any direct physical loss not excluded under the policy. The following perils are excluded under the policy:

- Wear and tear, Smog, Fungus, rust, corrosion, deterioration, and any innate defects, Mechanical breakdown
- Pollutant discharge (except when it is caused by a specific cause of loss), Insect, bird, or rodent damage
- Poor planning, development, design, workmanship, etc.
- Collapse not listed under collapse additional coverage
- Steam explosion (boilers, pipes, and engines)
- Settling, shrinking, expanding, and cracking
- Criminal or dishonest activities carried out by the insured or his employees
- Damage caused by decisions and actions
- Damage caused by failing to make correct decisions or act appropriately
- Damage to personal property located outside the building caused by rain, ice, or snow
- Fraudulent or deceitful acts that cause the insured to lose property

The cause of loss—special form includes the **limited mold additional coverage and the collapse additional coverage.**

The cause of loss—special form has the following coverage limitations:

- $2,500 limit on theft coverage for furs and garments lined with or made of fur
- $2,500 limit on theft coverage for dies, patterns, molds, and forms
- $2,500 limit on theft coverage for jewelry and watches worth more than $100, precious and semiprecious stones, jewels, gold, silver, and platinum
- $250 limit on theft coverage for stamps, credit letters, tickets, and lottery tickets for sale

To receive coverage, the following items must be damaged by a glass breakage or a cause of loss listed in the broad form:

- Valuable papers, records, storage media, drawings, and similar items
- Statuary, marble, porcelain, chinaware, and other fragile items
- Building machinery or equipment owned by the insured or in his care
- Animals that are killed

CONDITIONS FOUND ON HOMEOWNER'S POLICIES

Homeowner's policies include the following conditions: **other insurance, assignment, policy changes, liberalization, concealment or fraud, subrogation, policy period,** and **cancellation**. According to the cancellation condition, the insurer can cancel a policy under the following circumstances:

- The insurer can cancel for any reason within the initial 60 days of the policy period. Ten days written notice is required.
- The insured commits material misrepresentation. Thirty days written notice is required.
- The insured's risk level changes significantly. Thirty days written notice is required.
- The insured fails to pay premiums. Ten days written notice is required.
- The insurer can simply exercise its nonrenewal option at the end of the policy period.

SECTIONS OF AN INSURANCE CONTRACT

Insurance contracts are divided into the following sections:

- **Declaration** – This lists the identity of the insured, his or her address, the cost of the policy, a general description of the items being insured, and the coverage amount.
- **Insuring agreement** – This specifies the property being covered, its type, the perils against which it is protected, and the exact loss amount the insured will recover (indemnity).
- **Conditions** – This explains the responsibilities of both parties and the provisions they must fulfill.
- **Exclusions** – This identifies any losses or perils that are not covered (indemnified) by the contract.
- **Definitions** – This section defines and clarifies the terms found in the policy. These terms are often specific to the type of policy being issued.

CHARACTERISTICS OF AN INSURANCE CONTRACT

Adhesion indicates that one party has more power in drafting the contract than the other party. Insurance contracts are considered adhesive because the insurance provider writes contractual provisions with little or no input from the insured party, who simply agrees to the terms. Unfortunately, adhesive contracts often use ambiguous language. This can leave the insured party confused about the exact terms and conditions of the contract. In cases where ambiguity creates confusion, courts normally rule in favor of the insured.

Conditional contracts include provisions that both parties must fulfill. In the case of insurance contracts, the insured party alerts the insurance provider when a loss occurs. Then, the insurance provider must assess the damage and determine a value amount according to the methods set forth in the contract.

Personal contracts, such as insurance contracts, only insure people, not property. Consequently, if covered property is damaged, the contract only issues payments to a person.

Unilateral indicates that a contract is one-sided. Insurance contracts are unilateral because only the insurance provider is obligated to fulfill the contract. If a loss occurs, the insurer is legally required to issue payments. However, the insured can opt out of the contract at any time simply by ceasing to make payments.

Utmost good faith indicates that both parties involved in the contract are relying on their mutual integrity. For instance, an insurance contract is issued under the following assumptions: the insurance provider will fulfill its obligation to cover any losses, and the insured will be honest regarding any losses incurred.

CIRCUMSTANCES UNDER WHICH AN INSURANCE COMPANY CAN VOID A POLICY

Insurance companies have the right to void a policy if the any of the following activities are discovered:

- **Misrepresentation** – This can be either intentional or unintentional, and involves an applicant misstating a fact, either verbally or in writing. The policy can only be voided if the misrepresentation involves a **material fact**, which is any factor that would influence the company to reject an application or alter or raise the policy's premium.
- **Concealment** – This occurs when an applicant withholds material facts.

- **Fraud** – This is always intentional because it involves a deliberate deception that is harmful to the company. For an action to be considered fraud, the following elements must be present: an individual must intentionally lie in order to alter someone's decision; the individual's lie must result in the decision being altered; the lie must result in damage.

INSURANCE CONTRACT AND THE CRITERIA THAT MUST BE MET FOR THEM TO BE CONSIDERED LEGALLY VALID

An **insurance contract** is a legally binding agreement between an insurance provider and a party seeking insurance coverage. It obligates the provider to protect the insured against any losses associated with a certain risk event, such as theft or fire. Insurance contracts are only legally valid if they possess the following criteria:

- **Competency** – Both parties must conform to the legal definition of competency. Individuals working under the influence of chemical substances, the insane, and minors are excluded under the legal definition of competency.
- **Offer and acceptance**, also known as **agreement** – The contract must be offered by one party and accepted (or fulfilled) by the other.
- **Legal purpose** – The contract cannot be enforced if it violates any laws.
- **Consideration** – Both parties must agree on some type of compensation in exchange for the services provided. For instance, the insurance provider agrees to assume any liabilities or losses associated with a certain risk event.

UNDERWRITING DEPARTMENT

The goal of **underwriting** is to insure only those risks that are likely to fulfill the insurance provider's economic goals. The underwriting department evaluates the risk level of each application against a set standard. The personal judgment of the members of the underwriting department is also taken into account. Applications are normally rejected if their potential for loss outweighs their potential for gain. When making these decisions, underwriters consider the following ratios:

- **Loss Ratio** = Incurred Loss Amount / Earned Premium Amount
- **Expense Ratio** = Total Underwriting Expenses / Total Written Premiums
- **Combined Ratio** = Loss Ratio + Expense Ratio

The underwriting department also has the following responsibilities: identifying which policy forms are necessary to provide the coverage an applicant is seeking, evaluating loss experience, and offering judgment rates.

RATING A POLICY

After a company decides to insure an applicant, it must determine a premium amount for the policy. Premium rates are calculated using one of three possible methods: judgment rating, manual rating, and merit rating.

Judgment rating is the oldest method relying solely on expert judgment rather than tables. Underwriters simply assess the policy's risk level and determine a premium.

Manual rating, also known as **class rating**, is the most common method. Premium rates are organized by category and listed on a table. An underwriter analyzes the characteristics of the risk, and then classifies the risk according to the categories on the table. A premium is selected based on the corresponding category. The total premium is calculated by multiplying the rate by the number of insurance units. Consider, for instance, a person who purchases $500,000 of insurance at a listed rate of $5 per $2,500. The total premium would be $1,000.

CANCELING A POLICY

Policies can be cancelled in several different ways. If the insured wishes to cancel his policy, he can relinquish it or write a letter to the insurance provider. He then receives **unearned premiums**, which include any premiums that the policy has not yet used. Unearned premiums are often repaid on a **short rate basis**, which means that the company will keep a portion of the unused premiums to cover expenses. Insurance providers seldom have the same right to arbitrary cancellation that insureds have. In most states, companies can only cancel a policy if the insured is failing to pay the premiums. Furthermore, companies must provide the insured with written notification of cancellation, and must repay premiums on a **pro rata basis**, which indicates that the company is not allowed to keep any unused premiums for expenses. Another cancellation method is known as **flat cancellation**, which involves canceling the policy on its effective date.

FAIR CREDIT REPORTING ACT

According to the **Fair Credit Reporting Act**, credit reporting agencies must maintain a consumer's right to privacy, exercise their duties impartially, alert the consumer under certain circumstances, and update information that is old or false. The Fair Credit Reporting Act is important within the insurance industry because companies frequently hire credit reporting agencies to prepare credit reports on applicants. Credit reports are classified as either **consumer** or **investigative consumer**. These differ only in that investigative consumer reports involve personal interviews with the consumer's associates. Neither type of report can include bankruptcy information older than 10 years or legal actions older than 7 years. If an insurance company orders an investigative consumer report, it must send **initial written notice** to the applicant within three days of making the order. Consumers then have the right to request additional information, which must be sent in five days. They also have the right to challenge information included in the report. Additionally, if an insurance company raises rates or denies coverage, it must inform the applicant of the specific information that led to the decision.

Types of Casualty Policies and Bonds

COMMERCIAL PROPERTY INSURANCE AND THE CONTROL OF PROPERTY CONDITION

Commercial property insurance is part of the commercial package policy. It provides property insurance for businesses, and covers both real property (factories, buildings, etc.) and business personal property (machinery, inventory, desks, etc.). Commercial property insurance includes the following forms: **declarations, conditions, coverage, cause of loss** (basic, broad, and special), and **mandatory** and **optional endorsements**. Coverage forms identify property that is covered and not covered, and explain any limits, deductibles, and special conditions. They include the following types: building and personal property, builder's risk, extra expense, business income with extra expense, business income without extra expense, condominium association, and condominium commercial unit-owners.

Control of property condition is listed in the commercial property conditions form. It stipulates the following:

- The insurance policy will not be affected when a person commits an act of neglect without permission or direction from the insured.
- Policy violations by the insured at one location will not impact other insured locations.

COMMERCIAL GENERAL LIABILITY INSURANCE

Commercial general liability insurance (CGL) protects businesses against the following liability exposures:

- **Premises and operations** – This includes bodily injury, property damage, personal and advertising, and other types of liability inherent to conducting business in a certain location or carrying out certain business activities.
- **Products-completed operations** – This is the liability a business incurs through defective products or operations.
- **Indirect or contingent liability** – This is the liability a business incurs through the actions of others, such as agents, employees, and contractors.

The following liabilities are not included in CGL and require specific supplemental policies:

- Injuries to employees in the course of their work
- Liability the business may incur through contractual agreements
- Pollution
- Automobile, aircraft, and watercraft usage, maintenance, or ownership

Commercial general liability insurance policies consist of the following parts: common policy declarations, common policy conditions, CGL declarations, CGL coverage forms (which provide three standard coverages: A, B, and C), and mandatory endorsements.

COMMERCIAL GENERAL LIABILITY INSURANCE TERMS

Autos are vehicles designed solely for use on public roads, such as motor vehicles, trailers, and semi-trailers, as well as their attached machinery and equipment. Autos also include self-propelled vehicles attached to the following types of equipment: snow removal, street cleaning, road maintenance (except for resurfacing or construction), cherry pickers, air compressors, pumps, and generators.

78

Mobile equipment includes the following:

- Vehicles whose primary use is limited to locations off of public roads, such as farm machinery, forklifts, and bulldozers
- Vehicles used primarily on or around the insured's premises
- Vehicles that move on crawler treads
- Vehicles whose primary use is transporting shovels, power cranes, diggers, loaders, differs, drills, and road construction/resurfacing equipment
- Non-self propelled vehicles attached to air pumps, compressors, and cherry pickers
- Other types of vehicles whose primary use does not involve transporting people or cargo

A vehicle must be classified as either an auto or mobile equipment, never both. The two definitions do not overlap.

Insured's products are defined as any goods or services that the insured (including those operating under the insured's name and any business owned by the insured) sells, handles, distributes, manufactures, or disposes. This definition excludes real property, but includes the following:

- Equipment included with the product, such as parts and containers
- Any product warranties (such as perform, quality, fitness, etc.) and representations
- Any warning or instructions provided with or omitted from the product

Insured's work is defined as any work the insured or someone working under the insured's name performs, including the following:

- Any equipments, parts, or materials used in conjunction with the work
- Any warranties or representation regarding work quality or performance
- Any warnings or instructions that the insured provided or omitted regarding the work

Impaired property includes two types of tangible property: products or works of the insured that are believed to be defective, dangerous, or flawed, and products that do not conform to contractual requirements. Impaired property cannot be classified as the insured's products or work, but it must be repairable by an adjustment or repair of the insured's products or work.

Products-completed operations hazard is any bodily injury or property damage possessing the following characteristics:

- Sustained somewhere other than the insured's premises
- Occurs due to the insured's product or work, provided the product or work was not in the insured's physical possession and has not been completed or abandoned

Leased workers are acquired through a labor leasing firm. The insured signs an agreement with the firm, and obtains workers to perform certain duties.

Temporary workers either substitute for permanent employees who are absent or fill a specific seasonal or situational need.

Employees are people employed by the insured, including leased workers, but excluding temporary workers and volunteer workers.

Volunteer workers do not receive payment from the insured or his associates. They do not charge a fee for their work, and carry out job duties at the insured's discretion and direction.

Coverage territory is the area in which the commercial general liability insurance applies. This normally encompasses the U.S., any U.S. territories or possessions, Canada, and other described territories. International waters and airspace are also included if the injured party was traveling between the described territories when the injury occurred. The coverage territory can be extended worldwide if any one of the following situations is present:

- The injury was caused by goods or products created or sold within the described territory.
- The injury was the result of an illegal advertisement sent through the Internet.
- The injury was caused by someone who lives in the described territory who was performing work on the insured's behalf outside of the described territory.

In these situations, the insurance company will cover the liability of the insured if he is found legally responsible for damages.

Pollutants include smoke, soot, fumes, acid, chemicals, waste, and any other contaminant or irritant in a solid, liquid, gaseous, or thermal state.

Loading or unloading is performed in the following situations:

- Property is moved or loaded onto an aircraft, watercraft, or auto after it has been approved for such loading
- Property is moved around on or in the aircraft, watercraft, or auto
- Property is unloaded off of the aircraft, watercraft, or auto, and moved to its delivery location

If property is moved by a hand truck or similar mechanical device that is not part of the aircraft, watercraft, or auto, it does not fall under the definition of loading or unloading.

COMMERCIAL PROPERTY INSURANCE CONDITIONS

The **liberalization** condition applies when the insurance company revises the policy to broaden coverage and does not charge any additional premiums. If the insurer implemented the revision during the policy period or 45 days before the policy's effective date, the revised coverage automatically goes into effect.

According to the **legal action against us** condition, the insured has a maximum of two years following a direct physical loss to file a suit against the insurer. Legal action is only allowed if the insured has abided by all policy conditions.

The **other insurance** condition states the following:

- When another insurance policy is covering the same loss on the same basis, the policy reimburses its proportion of the loss.
- When another insurance policy is covering the same loss on a different plan, the policy reimburses any excess amount remaining after the other policy has paid up to its limits.

Under the **concealment or fraud** condition, if the insured knowingly misrepresents or conceals material facts related to property coverage or claims, all commercial property coverage outlined in the policy is voided.

The **policy period, coverage territory** condition holds that losses are only covered if they take place in the coverage territory during the policy period.

The **transfer of rights of recovery against others to us** grants subrogation rights to the insurer.

According to the **no benefit to bailee** condition, commercial property insurance will not reimburse a bailee, even if he is in possession of the insured property when it is damaged.

The **insurance under two or more coverages** condition states that if two coverages on the same policy apply to the same loss, the insurer is not obligated to reimburse more than the actual loss or damage amount.

COVERAGES A, B, AND C ON COMMERCIAL GENERAL LIABILITY INSURANCE

Coverage A—bodily injury and property damage liability reimburses the insured's liability expenses (including legal defense costs) when he is found legally responsible for bodily injury or property damage caused by an **occurrence**, also known as an **accident**. An injury results from an occurrence when it is caused by repeated or continuous contact with the same source of harm.

Coverage B—personal and advertising injury liability pays the insured's liability expenses when he is found legally responsible for libel or slander.

Coverage C—medical payments reimburses medical costs resulting from bodily injury, regardless of who was at fault. The injury must have occurred on or adjacent to the insured's premises or in conjunction with the insured's business activities. Additionally, the insured must report the injury to the insurance company within one year of the accident date. Otherwise, coverage does not apply.

All coverages are available on either occurrence forms or claims-made forms.

Coverage A excludes liabilities that result from the following:

- Intentional injury
- Signing a contract or agreement
- Maintaining or using autos, aircraft, or watercraft listed under the policy
- Government regulation of alcoholic beverages (if the insured is in the alcoholic beverage business)
- Work-related injuries already included under workers' compensation laws
- Pollution damage that causes bodily injury or property damage, or incurs clean-up costs

Coverage A excludes liabilities that result from the following:

- Damage sustained by the insured's products due to some innate defect
- Damage sustained by the insured's work
- Personal or advertising injury
- Transporting mobile equipment using an auto, preparing an auto for use in a prearranged race, or using an auto to participate in a prearranged race
- Product recalls due to some known or suspected defect within the product
- Defects and dangers inherent in the insured's products or work
- Nonconformance with contractual obligations
- Damage sustained by property that the insured owns, rents, occupies, or otherwise cares for, unless the property is being rented for less than seven consecutive days
- War or warlike activities that have been assumed under a contract

Coverage B excludes liabilities that result from the following:

- Willfully and illegally inflicting injury on another
- Contract breach
- Any publishing done prior to the policy's effective date
- Criminal activities committed or ordered by the insured
- Activities already covered under contract, unless the insured would have incurred the liability regardless of whether it was covered by a contract
- Listing incorrect prices for products and services
- Products and services failing to meet advertised quality standards
- Insured's business activities as a provider of Internet service, search, access, or search
- Insured's business activities as an advertiser, broadcaster, publisher, or designer of web content for others
- Insured's unauthorized use of another's name in email addresses, metatags, or domain names
- Insured's hosting, ownership, or control of an electronic chatroom or bulletin board
- Infringing upon the copyright, patent, intellectual properties, trademark, or trade secrets of others
- Any type of loss related to pollution

Coverage C excludes injuries from coverage if they are:

- Caused by war
- Excluded by Coverage A
- Already covered under workers' compensation laws
- Sustained by the insured, his employees, his tenants, or anyone who else who is occupying an area of the premises he usually occupies, unless they are volunteer workers
- Sustained while performing athletic activities
- Part of products-completed operations hazard under Coverage A

DIFFERENT DESIGNATIONS FOR NAMED INSUREDS IN THE DECLARATIONS SECTION

The declarations section of a commercial general liability insurance policy includes the following designations for named insureds:

- **Individual** – This includes the named insured and his spouse, and is only available for sole proprietorships.
- **Partnership or joint venture** – This includes the named insured, his members and their spouses (only when they are performing business-related duties), and his partners and their spouses (only when they are performing business-related duties).
- **Limited liability company** – This includes the named insured, his members (only when they are performing business-related duties), and his managers (only when they are performing management-related duties).
- **Organization other than partnership, joint venture, or limited liability company** – This includes the named insured, stockholders (only their liability as stockholders), and executive officers and directors (only when they are performing business-related duties).
- **Trust** – This includes the named insured and trustees (only when they are performing their trustee duties).

PEOPLE OTHER THAN THE NAMED INSURED WHO ARE COVERED

In addition to the named insured, commercial general liability policies also cover the following persons while they are performing duties for the named insured that are related to their jobs:

- Employees of the named insured, except for those included under named insured designations
- Volunteer workers
- Non-employees and organizations serving as real estate managers
- Persons or organizations with temporary custody of the named insured's property following the named insured's death (Coverage only applies to the liability associated with using the property, and only lasts until the estate appoints a legal representative.)
- The legal representative of the named insured after his death
- People and organizations responsible for driving the insured's equipment on a public highway with the insured's permission

LIMITS OF INSURANCE ON COMMERCIAL GENERAL LIABILITY POLICIES

General aggregate limit is the maximum total amount available for Coverages A, B, and C. Through endorsement, a separate general aggregate limit can be applied to each insured location and/or project. This limit does not include damages related to the products-completed operations hazard.

Products-completed operations aggregate limit is the maximum amount Coverage A pays out for damages related to the products-completed operations hazard.

Per occurrence limit is the maximum amount Coverages A and C will pay out for bodily injury, property damage, and medical payments in a single occurrence. This limit is part of either the general aggregate limit or the product-completed operations aggregate limit.

Personal and advertising injury limit is the maximum amount Coverage B will pay out for personal or advertising injury for one person or organization. This limit is included under the general aggregate limit.

Damage to premises rented to the insured limit is the maximum amount Coverage A will pay out for liability related to fire damage sustained by premises that the insured rents or occupies with permission from the owner. This limit applies on a per occurrence basis (one fire), and is part of the general aggregate limit and per occurrence limit.

Medical expense limit is the maximum amount Coverage C will pay out for medical expenses related to bodily injury to a single person. This limit is part of the general aggregate limit and per occurrence limit.

CONDITIONS ON COMMERCIAL GENERAL LIABILITY POLICIES

Your **right to claim and occurrence information condition** only applies to the claims-made form, not the occurrence form. It mandates that the insurance company must provide the named insured with the following information related to the existing claims-made forms and any other claims-made forms the company has given the insured over the previous three years:

- A listing of occurrences that the insured has reported only to his current insurer (according to policy provisions), not any other insurance company
- A yearly summary of money collected and reserved under both the general aggregate limit and the products-completed operations aggregate limit

83

ıst be provided when the following circumstances are present:

ıed insured sends a written request to the insurer within the 60 days following
:xpiration date. The insurer has a maximum of 45 days to provide the
after receiving the request.

canceled or not renewed by the insurance company. The insurer must provide
tion at least 30 days before the policy's expiration date.

The **other insurance condition** applies when the same loss is covered by both commercial general liability insurance (as the primary policy) and other insurance. It states that the loss can be settled using either the **contribution by equal shares method** or the **contribution by limits method**.

The declarations sections of commercial general liability policies provide automatic coverage for new organizations acquired or created by the insured if the new organization is:

- Not covered by any other insurance.
- Owned or under majority control by the insured.

Coverage lasts for 90 days or until the end of the policy period, whichever option represents the least amount of time. However, the insured can extend coverage by reporting the new organization to the insurer. Coverage only applies to losses sustained after the organization was obtained.

Pollution liability coverage extension endorsement provides coverage for bodily injury and property damage. It negates Coverage A's exclusion on those types of damages. Pollution cleanup costs are not covered.

Liquor liability coverage form is available for those in the liquor business, and covers the liabilities associated with selling liquor.

Owner's and contractor's protective liability coverage form covers any liability the insured may incur from the activities of independent contractors. In most cases, someone other than the named insured purchases this form to cover the insured.

Pollution liability coverage form reimburses the damage and cleanup costs resulting from pollution emissions onto insured property. The **pollution liability-limited coverage form** provides the same coverage minus cleanup costs. Pollution forms are available on a claims-made basis only. The other forms are available on both a claims-made and occurrence basis.

PERSONAL AUTO INSURANCE

Personal auto insurance is a personal, multi-line (property and casualty) policy. Insurers can issue auto policies either on an individual basis or a joint basis to husbands and wives living in the same household. In many states, the insured is legally required to have auto insurance. In every state, the insured must have a minimum coverage limit on certain types of liability if he has been in an accident, has been found guilty of a serious traffic offense, or was unable to pay a fine from a previous traffic offense. These limits vary from state to state. For instance, some states mandate 20/40/15 coverage: $20,000 for bodily injury per person per accident, $40,000 for bodily injury per accident, and $15,000 for property damage per accident. Personal auto policies also offer property insurance, which protects the insured against property damage resulting from collision and non-collision losses.

Personal Auto Policy, or **PAP**, is a basic type of auto insurance, containing a declarations section and a policy form. It includes four essential coverages, each of which has unique insuring agreements, conditions, and exclusions:

- **Part A**—Liability Coverage
- **Part B**—Medical Payments Coverage
- **Part C**—Uninsured Motorist Coverage
- **Part D**—Coverage for (Physical) Damage to Your Auto

The insured is not required to purchase all coverages. However, state laws may dictate which coverages he must have. For instance, Part A is always a requirement, while Part B is usually optional. A PAP covers **private passenger autos**, which include vehicles identified in the declarations section, as well as new vehicles acquired during the policy period, **temporary substitute autos**, and **trailers**.

PERSONAL AUTO POLICY ENDORSEMENTS

Towing and labor costs endorsement provides a minimum of $25 for the towing and labor costs that are incurred when a vehicle is disabled. Labor is only reimbursed if it is performed at the place where the vehicle was disabled.

Miscellaneous type vehicle endorsement covers vehicles that are not normally insured by the policy, such as motorcycles, mopeds, motor homes, and golf carts. Not all companies offer this endorsement. The insured may have to purchase a separate **specialized** policy to cover these vehicles.

Extended non-owner coverage endorsement provides coverage for the insured and his family, even when they are operating vehicles not owned by the insured or excluded under the basic policy, such as work vehicles.

Optional limits transportation expenses coverage endorsement reimburses the insured for transportation and/or loss of uses expenses incurred when a scheduled or non-owned auto is disabled. The insured chooses the limits (daily and maximum) of this coverage.

PARTS A, B, C, D, E, AND F OF AUTO POLICIES

Part A—Liability Coverage insures the policyholder against bodily injury and property damage for which he is legally liable. This coverage does not apply unless the insured is legally responsible for injuring or damaging the property of another person, the injuries and damages are covered under the policy, and the loss is caused by an auto accident. Under most circumstances, Part A insures the following groups:

- The named insured and his or her family when they are operating any automobile
- Any person operating the insured's car, if he has received permission from the insured
- Any other person or organization who shares liability with the insured
- Any other person or organization who incurs liability from operating an automobile or trailer owned by the insured and his family

The policy reimburses any damages or settlements up to the limit of liability. In addition to this limit, the policy also pays any defense costs and prejudgment interest. Once the limit has been reached, however, the insurer is not obligated to pay any additional expenses.

The **out of state coverage** provision insures covered autos being driven through multiple states. It guarantees the Personal Auto Policy will fulfill the financial responsibility and legal requirements of any state through which the auto is driven.

According to the **other insurance** clause, when a vehicle is covered by multiple insurers, the insurer is only obligated to pay its portion of the loss. This portion is determined by dividing the liability limit of the insurer's policy by the total liability limit of all policies. For instance, assume a single auto is covered by two policies: policy A and policy B. Policy A has a liability limit of $40,000, while policy B has a limit of $30,000. If an accident occurs, policy A will reimburse 57% ($40,000/$70,000) of the liability damages. The other insurance clause only applies when the insured is driving a vehicle owned by him.

Part B—Medical Payments Coverage reimburses any reasonable medical expenses incurred when the named insured, his or her family members, or passengers are injured in an auto accident. Part B is not liability coverage. Rather, it applies no matter who is at fault, and covers medical and funeral costs for the following parties for a maximum of three years following the date of the accident:

- The named insured and his or her family members, whether they are occupants of autos and trailers intended for public road use or pedestrians hit by such vehicles
- Another person who is occupying the named insured's vehicle with the insured's permission

The insured cannot collect duplicate payments under Part B if a loss is already covered elsewhere in the policy. Also, the other insurance condition under Part B is identical to the other insurance condition under Part A.

Part B provides a single limit of liability. In effect, one limit (usually $1,000, $2,000, $5,000, $10,000, or even $100,000) covers each person per accident.

Part C—Uninsured Motorists Coverage protects the insured when he is involved in an auto accident with an uninsured or underinsured person. It reimburses certain losses that would have been covered by the other person's insurance. Bodily injury is normally the only loss covered by Part C. Punitive damages are never covered. Part C insures the following persons: the named insured and his or her family; any person occupying the covered auto; any person who has the right to recover BI damages for the injured party when the injury is caused by an uninsured motorist (such as a parent who is reimbursed the medical expenses of a child involved in an accident). A loss must meet the following four conditions before Part C takes effect:

- There must be an auto accident resulting in bodily injury.
- The insured must incur a loss.
- The insured must have a legal entitlement to collect bodily injury damages.
- The other driver must fulfill the definition of an uninsured motor vehicle.

Part C's limit of liability is either a **single limit** (one limit covering every type of loss) or a **split limit** (a separate limit for each type of loss). Part C does not cover losses in the following situations:

- They have already been reimbursed on behalf of the responsible party (duplicate coverage).
- They are also covered by workers' compensation or disability benefits.

According to the **other insurance** clause, when multiple Personal Auto Policies are covering the same person, the maximum insurance limit cannot exceed the Part C limit of the largest single policy. For instance, assume that a person is insured by three separate Personal Auto Policies. Policy 1 has a Part C limit of $300,000, policy 2 has a Part C limit of $250,000, and policy 3 has a Part C limit of $100,000. In the event of an accident with an uninsured motorist, the insured cannot collect more than $300,000 because policy 1 has the largest single Part C limit.

Part D—Coverage for Damage to Your Auto insures against physical damage to vehicles owned or used by the insured. This coverage only applies when the loss is direct and accidental, and caused by the following:

- Collision
- Other than collision, or OTC

In essence, Part D provides open peril protection, but only covers the vehicle and its attached components. It does not apply to any personal property stored within the vehicle. Part D also offers **transportation expense coverage**, which pays the insured $20 per day (up to a $600 maximum limit) when he incurs the following expenses:

- Transportation expenses due to physical damage or loss to the insured's auto, as long as the damage is covered under collision and OTC.
- Loss of use expenses resulting from any legal liability the insured may incur as a result of damage to an auto he does not own.
- Transportation expenses due to theft of the insured's auto – In this situation, there is a 48-hour waiting period before coverage is provided.

The collision and OTC coverages protect the insured against physical damage to his vehicle. Physical damage loss is reimbursed by paying the **actual cash value** or the **repair/replacement value**, whichever is lesser. **Collision** coverage applies when the insured's vehicle collides with another object or vehicle. **Other than collision** (or **OTC**) coverage applies when the insured's vehicle sustains virtually any other type of direct and accidental loss not excluded under the policy. OTC coverage protects against the following kinds of perils: glass breakage; fire; water, flood, and hail; windstorm; theft or larceny; riot; bird or animal contact; explosion; earthquake; malicious mischief and vandalism; and falling objects such as missiles. The insured does not have to purchase both kinds of coverage, and can even use different coverages for different cars. Part D also provides coverage for **temporary substitute autos** and **non-owned autos**, which are defined as any autos not owned by the insured. For each occurrence covered under collision coverage or OTC coverage, there is a separate deductible.

Part D excludes the following types of damages from coverage:

- Freezing, wear and tear, electrical/mechanical breakdown, and road wear on tires
- Nuclear or war-related activities
- Government destruction or confiscation of property (The interests of a loss payee are still covered.)
- Participation in a prearranged contest, such as a race
- Radar, laser, and other types of detection equipment
- Usage as public or livery transportation
- Usage for business-related activities (The named insured and his family members are covered as long as they are using private passenger autos or trailers.)

- Usage as part of an auto business
- Usage of a non-owned auto by the named insured or his family if they lack permission or entitlement to do so

Part D excludes the following types of property from coverage:

- All visual, audio, and data electronic equipment, such as radios, CD players, tape players, PCs, phones, VCRs, and videos, including their parts and accessories (This type of equipment is not excluded if it is permanently installed in the auto or operated by the auto's electrical system via a detachable housing unit.)
- Trailers, campers, and motor homes, including their refrigeration, dining, cooking, and plumbing equipment, if they are not included in the declaration section (If the trailer is not owned by the insured, it is not excluded from coverage.)
- Any type of equipment intended to expand living space, such as awnings and cabanas
- Custom furnishings and similar equipment in pickups and vans (Caps, bedliners, and covers are covered.)
- An auto that a named insured or his family member is renting, as long as state laws or the rental agreement prohibits the rental agency from collecting from the insured or his family member.

The **other sources of recovery** provision applies when there are multiple auto policies covering the same person. It is very similar to the other insurance condition under Parts A and B of auto policies, but there is one major exception, which is that if a loss occurs, the insurer will factor in every source of recovery (even sources other than insurance) when determining what percentage of the loss it owes.

According to **the no benefit to bailee** condition, if an insured auto is damaged while in the possession of a bailee (such as a repair shop or parking garage); the bailee cannot receive any insurance benefit.

According to **Part E—Duties After an Accident or Loss**, the insured must perform the following duties after a loss:

- Notify the police as soon as possible if the loss involved a hit-and-run accident (according to uninsured motorist coverage) or theft
- Take reasonable precautions to safeguard his auto and related property against additional damage (according to physical damage coverage)
- Allow the insurance company to assess the damage before it determines whether repairing or disposing of the property is the best course of action

Named non-owner coverage endorsement provides coverage for persons who rent (or borrow) rather than own their auto. This endorsement automatically covers private passengers, pickups, panel trucks, and vans for 14 days if they were acquired during the policy period.

Joint ownership coverage endorsement enables an auto policy to be issued to two or more people living in the same household, even if they are not husband and wife.

Part F—General Provisions explains coverage conditions of the policy, including the duties and obligations of both the insured and the insurer. These conditions, duties, and obligations include the following:

- Losses are covered only when they occur during the policy period and inside the policy territory.
- The insured can only take legal action against the insurer if all policy terms have been fulfilled, and can never sue to determine liability for a loss.
- The insurer must provide written endorsement before changing or waiving policy terms.
- Subrogation rights are granted to the insurer unless the loss involves a person who is operating a covered auto with permission or entitlement to do so.
- The termination condition explains the cancellation and nonrenewal requirements for both the insured and the insurer.

The termination condition under Part F (General Provisions) explains the requirements for canceling or not renewing an auto policy. Although the insured can cancel on any date by providing written notice, the insurer is bound by far more stringent cancellation rules. Within the first 60 days of a new policy period, the insurer is subject to the following requirements:

- It must provide 10 days written notice if it is canceling because the insured is failing to pay premiums.
- It must provide 20 days written notice if it is canceling for some other reason.

After the first 60 days of a new policy period, the insurer can only cancel under the following conditions:

- The insured is failing to pay premiums.
- The insured has misrepresented material facts within the policy.
- The license of the insured vehicle's driver has been revoked or suspended.

Additionally, insurers must provide 20 days written notice if they do not intend to renew the policy.

LIABILITY INSURANCE

Parties often find themselves liable when another person suffers bodily injury or property damage. Consequently, many parties purchase **liability insurance**, which covers any legal defense costs or damages resulting from such injuries. Different types of liability insurance cover different categories of liability exposure. These categories include the following:

- **General liability** – covers the usage and maintenance of a property and the operation of a business.
- **Personal liability** – covers the activities of a person and his or her family when those activities are not business related.
- **Professional liability** – covers the liabilities associated with a particular profession
- **Business liability** – covers business conduct.
- **Advertising liability** – covers personal injuries (libel, slander, copyright infringement, privacy violations, etc.) resulting from advertising.
- **Vicarious liability** – This covers damages incurred as a result of one person's legal responsibility for another person or animal. For instance, parents can be held liable if their children vandalize another person's property.
- **Strict (absolute) liability** – This covers injuries resulting from dangerous practices and defective products. Negligence is not a consideration with this type of liability.

INJURIES AND DAMAGES THAT LIABILITY INSURANCE PAYS ON BEHALF OF THE INSURED

Bodily injury includes any bodily harm, disease, sickness, service loss, income loss, and/or death caused by an accident or occurrence for which the insured is liable.

Personal injury includes any mental or emotional anguish caused by the following: incarceration, false arrest, malicious prosecution, slander, defamation, libel, invasion of privacy, and/or wrongful eviction or entry.

Property damage includes property that has been damaged or destroyed. It also includes physical property that has not been damaged, but has sustained a loss of use.

Advertising injury includes the following:

- Oral and written statements slandering or libeling the goods, products, or services of an individual or organization
- Oral and written statements infringing upon an individual's right to privacy
- Advertising ideas or business methods that have been misappropriated
- Copyright or trademark infringement

UNINSURED MOTOR VEHICLE

A motor vehicle is considered uninsured if it meets the following criteria:

- It is without liability coverage when the accident occurs.
- It has insufficient liability coverage according to state laws.
- Its liability coverage is invalid because the insurer has denied coverage or has suffered insolvency.
- Its driver is unidentified after committing a hit-and-run against the insured, his family members, the insured auto, or any motor vehicle occupied by the insured or his family.

A motor vehicle cannot be considered uninsured if any of the following criteria are present: the vehicle is owned by or regularly used by the insured or his family members; the vehicle is owned by the government; the vehicle is owned or used by a self-insured person (unless he suffers insolvency); the vehicle is used as a residence; the vehicle is intended for off road use; the vehicle is run on crawler treads or rails.

UNDERINSURED MOTORIST'S COVERAGE ENDORSEMENT AND ASSIGNED RISK PLANS

Underinsured motorist's coverage is a type of liability endorsement available on auto policies. It applies when the insured is in an auto accident with a motorist whose coverage meets state requirements (meaning the motorist cannot be considered uninsured), but is insufficient to cover all the insured's losses. This coverage reimburses the difference between the actual loss amount and the amount paid out by the motorist's insurance. Depending on state law, it may be required or optional.

An **assigned risk plan**, also known as an **automobile insurance plan**, helps persons who are especially bad risks get auto insurance coverage (mainly bodily injury and property damage liability) that is sufficient to fulfill state law. Under an assigned risk plan, multiple insurance companies in the same state voluntarily pool their resources, and each company is assigned high-risk drivers at random.

COMMERCIAL AUTO INSURANCE

Commercial auto insurance provides liability and physical damage coverage for the insured business when it sustains a loss involving autos that it owns or uses. Commercial auto insurance policies include the following sections:

- Common policy declarations
- Common policy conditions
- Any number of five possible coverage forms (business auto, business auto physical damage, garage, truckers, or motor carriers)
- Corresponding declarations sections for the chosen coverage forms

Drive other car—broadened coverage for named individuals endorsement provides coverage for autos the named insured is using, not only autos he owns, hires, or borrows. This endorsement is not available for people actually named in the endorsement or their family members.

Individual named insured endorsement provides coverage for any auto that the named insured's immediate family members personally use. Coverage under this endorsement is almost identical to a Personal Auto Policy.

Employees as additional insureds endorsement covers autos that an employee is using on behalf of the named insured or his business, but are not owned, rented, or borrowed by the named insured.

Additional insured—lessor endorsement covers leased vehicles.

Specified hired autos endorsement provides the same coverage for scheduled hired autos that is provided for autos owned by the named insured.

Mobile equipment endorsement covers any mobile equipment as if it were an auto.

BUSINESS AUTO COVERAGE FORMS

Business Auto coverage forms reimburse the following expenses: any legal costs the insured may incur due to bodily injury or property damage resulting from owning, maintaining, or using a covered auto; defense costs for the insured; covered pollution costs or expenses (including liability), provided the accident involves a covered auto and includes both bodily injury and property damage. Business Auto coverage forms also provide the following supplementary payments, which are paid in addition to the limits of insurance:

- $2,000 maximum for bail bonds costs incurred due to a covered accident
- Bonds to release attachments (not to exceed the limits of insurance)
- Expenses incurred by the insured as a result of a lawsuit
- Costs the insured pays at the insurance company's behest (This supplementary payment provides a maximum of $250 for lost earnings)
- Postjudgment interest
- Other expenses the insured may incur

Business Auto coverage forms exclude the following liabilities from coverage:

- Injuries expected or intended by the insured
- Damages resulting from completed operations
- Contractual obligations for war and war-like acts

- Pollution damage that is not specifically listed in the policy
- Bodily injury and property damage caused by self-propelled vehicles with cherry pickers, pumps, generators, air compressors, and similar permanently attached equipment
- Covered autos used or being prepared for organized competitions
- Employees who sustain work-related injuries
- Property damage incurred when the property is being moved by a mechanical device
- Property covered under a previous contract or agreement, unless the liability would not have been incurred in the absence of a contract
- Property damage when the insured owns, transports, or controls the property

Business Auto coverage forms cover the named insured, as well as several other persons who are not technically considered insureds, such as:

- Owners of autos that employees or their families are renting or borrowing
- Persons working for an auto business
- Persons who are not employees or lessees transferring covered property to and from covered autos

The **out of state coverage extension** applies when business autos are driven through more than one state. It alters the commercial auto insurance coverage to conform to a particular state's liability requirements.

Worldwide liability coverage applies when the insured hires, rents, borrows, or leases a private passenger auto. It provides worldwide liability coverage for such a vehicle when it is obtained **without** a driver.

Covered pollution cost or expense describes pollution-related expenses that the insured must pay according to government regulations. These expenses will cover testing, monitoring, removing, treating, containing, detoxifying, neutralizing, or otherwise handling pollutants that have seeped into the insured's business. This coverage does not apply to the following:

- Pollutants that escape as they are being transported by the insured (including towing, handling, storing, disposing, processing, or treating) via a covered auto
- Pollutants that escape before they are moved into a covered auto from a specified place and after they are delivered

Diminution of value occurs when the property undergoes an actual or perceived reduction in market value or resale value. It is caused by a direct, accidental loss.

On Business Auto coverage forms, covered autos are designated primarily by their numbers:

1. **Any auto**—This includes autos used, owned, leased, hired, rented, or borrowed by the insured (liability coverage only).
2. **Owned autos only**—This includes autos owned by the insured.
3. **Owned primary passenger autos only**—This includes private passenger autos owned by the insured.
4. **Owned autos other than private passenger autos only**—This includes any trucks, buses, motorcycles, trailers, and similar vehicles owned by the insured.
5. **Owned autos subject to no-fault law**—This is used for autos that must have no-fault benefits under state law.

6. **Owned autos subject to compulsory uninsured motorists law**—This is used for autos that must have uninsured motorist coverage under state law.
7. **Specifically described autos**—This is reserved for vehicles identified in the declarations section.
8. **Hired autos only**—This is reserved for autos that have been hired, borrowed, or rented by the insured.
9. **Non-owned autos only**—This is reserved for autos that are used in the insured's business, but not hired, borrowed, or rented by the insured (liability coverage only).

Comprehensive coverage insures against any loss, provided it does not result from collision, overturn, or a cause specifically excluded by the policy. Standard deductibles include $500 and $1,000.

Specified cause of loss coverage provides named peril protection against the following causes of loss: fire, earthquake, flood, explosion, hail, lightning, theft, vandalism or mischief, windstorm, and, burning, collision, sinking, or derailment of a transport that is carrying a covered auto. There is only one deductible for this coverage: $25 for vandalism or mischief.

Collision coverage applies when a covered auto is overturned or collides with another object. Standard deductibles include $500 and $1,000. In some instances, glass breakage is reimbursed as a collision loss rather than a comprehensive loss, thereby negating the possibility of paying two deductibles when a collision causes both glass breakage and another type of damage.

Business Auto coverage forms offer the following extensions:

- **Transportation expenses coverage extension** – This provides $20 per day ($600 maximum) to cover the insured's transportation expenses after his auto is stolen. Reimbursement begins 48 hours after the auto is stolen, and ends once the auto has been returned or the insurer repays the loss.
- **Loss of use for rented autos coverage extension** –This provides $20 per day ($600 maximum) to cover loss of use for rented autos for which the insured is legally liable.

Business Auto coverage forms exclude losses from coverage if they result from the following:

- War
- Nuclear hazards
- Value diminution
- Tapes, records, and other sound reproducing or receiving equipment
- Natural wear and tear, mechanical/electrical breakdown, freezing, and tire damage from road use
- Participation in or preparation for a professional racing event or contest

Under the **settling physical damage claims** condition, the insurer offers three possible methods of reimbursing physical damage claims:

- Repair, replace, or repay the damaged or lost property. (If the property is completely lost, it is reimbursed at actual cash value minus depreciation. The insured must pay for any repair or replacement that exceeds the property's value before the damage occurred.)
- Return the stolen property and repair any damage.
- Appraise the damaged or stolen property and provide reimbursement at an agreed-upon value.

More than one policy coverage form condition states that, when multiple policies are covering the same loss, the insured cannot be reimbursed more than the highest single policy limit.

Legal action against the insurance company condition prevents the insured from suing the insurance company unless he has met all policy terms. For lawsuits stemming from liability, the insurer must pay any judgment amount determined after the trial.

According to the **other insurance condition**, Business Auto coverage forms are either:

- The primary coverage for accidents involving covered autos that the insured owns, and for liability arising out of covered trailers connected to covered autos that the insured owns.
- The excess coverage for accidents involving non-owned autos and non-owned trailers hooked to non-owned autos.

A Business Auto coverage form only pays its proportion of the loss when it and another form are covering the same loss.

GARAGE COVERAGE FORMS

Garage coverage forms provide **liability coverage**, **garagekeepers coverage**, and **physical damage coverage** for car dealerships, gas stations, parking garages, and other types of auto businesses. Covered autos are classified using the following designations:

- **Symbol 30** – This includes customer autos that the insured is keeping for the purposes of service, safe storage, or repair.
- **Symbol 31** – This covers dealer autos, including autos held for sale by the dealer, against physical damage.

Garage forms provide the following types of auto and business liability coverage:

- **Garage operation—covered autos** – This applies to owning, using, or maintaining covered autos. This coverage is identical to the Business Auto form coverage, except that garage customers with their own liability insurance are not covered.
- **Garage operations—other than covered autos** – This applies to operating a garage, and includes the named insured as well as his employees, business directors, and shareholders as they are carrying out their duties in the business.

Endorsements are available for uninsured motorists, underinsured motorists, and medical payments.

Garage physical damage coverage applies to either comprehensive or specific causes of loss and collision policies, and is normally purchased on a blanket basis so that it covers all vehicles the insured owns, regardless of whether or not each vehicle is specified. As a blanket coverage, garage physical damage excludes the following losses:

- Expected profits
- Collision damage for autos, if the collision occurs when the insured is transporting the auto between the purchase/distribution point to the destination point and the distance between the two points is 50 miles or more

Any type of garage physical damage coverage automatically excludes losses due to **false pretenses**, which occur when a dealer is tricked or deceived into giving away a covered auto.

GARAGEKEEPERS INSURANCE SECTION

The **garagekeepers insurance section** provides liability coverage for damage to others' property (including customer autos) when it is in the insured's control or custody for the purposes of service, parking, storage, or repair. This coverage is excluded under the form's regular liability section, and is part of symbol 30. **Direct damage garagekeepers insurance** is also available under this section. It reimburses losses that are incurred when the property of others is physically damaged, even when the insured is not legally liable for the damage. Direct damage garagekeepers insurance can be purchased on either a primary basis or an excess basis, and it can cover losses on either comprehensive or specified causes of loss and collision policies.

TRUCKERS COVERAGE FORMS

Truckers coverage forms apply to vehicles used by trucking businesses (those businesses that are hired to transport goods for others), and provide the following coverages:

- Liability coverage, similar to Business Auto forms.
- Physical damage coverage, similar to Business Auto forms.
- Trailer interchange coverage, which insures against losses to trailers that the named insured has hired or borrow (This coverage is only applicable if the loss was caused by a covered peril and the trucker signed a written interchange agreement.)

Covered autos are classified under the following designations:

- **Symbol 48** – This includes trailers that the named insured is borrowing or leasing under a written trailer interchange agreement, which obligates him to assume liability for loss.
- **Symbol 49** – This includes trailers that the named insured owns or has hired, but are in the possession of someone else under a written trailer interchange agreement.

MOTOR CARRIER COVERAGE FORMS AND THE MOTOR CARRIER ACT OF 1980

Motor carrier coverage forms contain virtually the same coverages as trucker's forms, but have a much broader application. They are available to any person who carries property in an auto as part of a business, even if he has not been hired expressly to transport goods. These forms provide trailer interchange coverage and coverage for private passenger autos.

According the **Motor Carrier Act of 1980**, trucking companies and motor carriers must be able to prove they can fulfill any financial liabilities resulting from injury or damage related to their business. The named insured must acquire the **MCS-90 endorsement** in situations where insurance is necessary to demonstrate financial responsibility. The limits of insurance are established by the weight of the vehicles and the property they are transporting.

BUILDING AND PERSONAL PROPERTY COVERAGE FORM

The **building and personal property coverage form** is the most common type of commercial property insurance form. It provides **building coverage** for the following: buildings, completed additions, outdoor furniture, floor coverings, select appliances, fixtures, personal property designed to maintain and protect the premises, additions, alterations, and repairs made during the construction process, and materials and supplies used to construct the building. This form also provides **business personal property coverage** for the following:

- Personal property used in the business
- Personal property of others that is in the insured's custody on the business premises
- Fixtures

- Machinery and equipment
- Furniture
- Personal property leased by the insured
- Stock (including the insured's merchandise, raw materials, manufacturing materials, and packaging and shipping supplies)
- Improvements and betterments (These must be made to a building that is occupied but not owned by the insured at the insured's expense. Also, the insured must be unable to legally remove them)

The building and personal property form excludes the following types of property from coverage:

- Money, securities, foods stamps, and similar monetary property
- Contraband, paved surfaces (roads, bridges, walks, etc.)
- Animals **not** being boarded or sold
- Airborne or waterborne personal property
- Electronic data (unless included under additional coverages)
- Repair/replacement cost of lost electronic or paper-based information (unless included under additional coverages)
- Property covered and explained more specifically under another policy
- Building/structure/machinery foundations below ground or basement level, Land excavation costs
- Autos being sold, land, water, etc.
- Docks, piers, pilings, bulkheads, and wharves
- Retaining walls not listed under the declarations section
- Pipes, drains, and flues situated underground
- Property located outside of buildings, such as crops, fences, antennas, signs, trees, shrubs, and plants (unless included under additional coverages)
- Vehicles used on public roads or beyond the premises, unless the insured is housing, manufacturing, or selling them, or they are rowboats or canoes in storage

BUILDING AND PERSONAL PROPERTY ADDITIONAL COVERAGES

Debris removal reimburses the cost of removing debris (except for pollutants) from covered property, provided the debris was the result of a covered loss. The reimbursement amount is equal to the deductible plus 25% of the amount paid to cover the direct loss to the property. The insurer will provide an additional $10,000 for debris removal under the following circumstances:

- The cost of debris removal is more than 25% of the amount paid to cover the direct loss.
- The combined costs of debris removal and direct loss exceed the limit of insurance.

Preservation of property insures property that has been removed from the insured location for the purposes of protecting it from a covered peril. This property is covered for a maximum of 30 days once it has been moved to the new location.

Pollutant cleanup and removal reimburses the cost of extracting pollutants from the insured premises when their presence is the result of a covered loss. This additional coverage only applies if the insured submits an expense report within 180 days of the loss. Reimbursement is limited to $10,000 plus the policy's limit.

Increased cost of construction applies after a covered loss has damaged a building. It pays the additional construction costs necessary to bring the structure into compliance with new building codes. This additional coverage does not cover any construction, testing, or removal costs related to the presence or effects of mold. Only buildings insured at replacement cost can receive this additional coverage, and the maximum reimbursement amount is the lesser of 5% of the building insurance amount or $10,000.

Fire department service charge reimburses a maximum of $1,000 (in addition to the limits of insurance) for payment of fire department services.

Electronic data reimburses the cost of replacing or restoring electronic data after it has been damaged or destroyed due to a covered cause of loss, including collapse and viruses. For insurance purposes, electronic data is defined as any information or computer program (except for prepackaged software) stored on computer software, hard/floppy disks, CD-ROMs, and similar kinds of electronic storage equipment. Losses are valued at the cost necessary to replace the damaged storage media with an identical blank storage media. The maximum reimbursement amount cannot exceed $2,500 for all electronic data losses incurred during one policy year. If a single loss occurs over multiple years, it is covered as if the entire loss occurred during the year in which it started.

BUILDING AND PERSONAL PROPERTY COVERAGE EXTENSIONS

Newly acquired or constructed property extends $250,000 of coverage for each new building the insured constructs at the covered premises or acquires for uses outlined in the declarations section. This extension also provides $100,000 of coverage for business personal property (both insured and newly acquired) stored at the new location. Coverage is limited to 30 days.

Property off-premises provides $10,000 for covered property that is temporarily stored at the following locations: locations not owned or leased by the insured, locations leased by the insured, and fairs, exhibitions, and trade shows.

Personal effects and property of others extends $2,500 of coverage for the personal property of others and personal effects owned by the named insured, his partners, or his employees. This extension does not cover theft. The insured can receive this extension without purchasing personal property of others coverage.

The **valuable papers and records—other than electronic data** extension insures papers and non-electronic records. It provides $2,500 when such documents are damaged and the information contained in them must be repaired or replaced.

The **outdoor property** extension covers fences, antennas, signs, satellite dishes, trees, plants, and shrubs on a limited basis ($1,000 maximum and a $250 limit per tree, shrub, or plant).

The **non-owned detached trailers** extension covers trailers that the insured does not own, but is legally liable for. The coverage does not apply when the trailer is connected to another vehicle, or is in the process of being connected to or disconnected from another vehicle. Coverage is normally limited to $5,000, but higher limits may be available.

BUILDING AND PERSONAL PROPERTY COVERAGE CONDITIONS

According to the **duties in the event of a loss condition**, the insured must perform the following duties after a loss:

- Provide the insurer with prompt notification of the loss, including a description of the damaged property and nature of the damage.
- Alert the police in the event of criminal activity.
- Safeguard the property against any more damage, and record the expenditures necessary to safeguard the property.
- Produce a complete inventory when required by the insurer.
- Facilitate the insurer's efforts to examine the damaged property, retrieve property samples, and look at books and records.
- Provide legal testimony of the loss at the insurer's request.
- Produce a signed sworn statement of loss if required by the insurer.

According to the **vacancy condition**, if the building has been vacant for longer than 60 consecutive days, the insurer is not obligated to cover losses resulting from theft, vandalism, water damage, sprinkler leakage, and glass breakage, and will reimburse all other covered losses at only 85% of their full value.

Mortgage condition protects the interests of any mortgage holders listed in the declarations section. It agrees to pay their losses and provide written notice in the event of policy cancellation. Ten days' notice is required if the insurer cancels due to nonpayment of premiums or decides not to renew the policy. Thirty days' notice is required if the insurer cancels for any other reason.

The **loss payment condition** mandates that once the insurer receives the insured's sworn statement of loss, it has 30 days to notify the insured of the settlement method that will be used.

BUILDING AND PERSONAL PROPERTY OPTIONAL COVERAGES

Building and personal property forms offer the following optional coverages:

- **Agreed value** optional coverage waives the coinsurance requirement, and requires the insurer to reimburse the loss at the proportion at which the limit of insurance holds to the stated value.
- **Inflation guard** optional coverage increases the policy's limit of insurance on an annual basis. The yearly increase in coverage will be a percentage (such as 7%) that both the insured and the insurer agree upon.
- Under the **replacement cost** optional coverage, covered property losses are reimbursed at **replacement cost** rather than actual cash value, which is the standard method used. Certain types of property listed under the declarations section are exempt from this coverage.

In order to activate these coverages, the insured must pay additional premiums.

BUILDER'S RISK COVERAGE FORM

The **builder's risk coverage form** insures commercial, residential, and farm buildings as they are being constructed. It covers the building and foundation, as well as any fixtures, machinery, or maintenance equipment, provided they are being permanently installed and are located within 100 feet of the structure. A coverage extension of $5,000 is available for building materials and supplies that are not owned by the insured, but are in his care. If the building has no basement, the builder's risk form goes into effect on the first day of construction. However, if the building does include a basement, it goes into effect when construction on the floor immediately above the basement begins. Coverage ends under the following circumstances:

- The coverage period expires (this happens after one year).
- Ninety days passes from the date construction ends.
- The insured no longer possesses an interest in the property.
- Construction is stopped and there is no intention to resume.
- The building begins fulfilling its intended use.

According to the **valuation condition**, builder's risk coverage reimburses losses at actual cash value, which is equal to the estimated worth of the building once it has been completed. **Need for adequate insurance condition** states that, in the event of a loss, the insurer will not reimburse an amount that is higher than the proportion that the limit of insurance holds to the completed building's estimated value. For instance, assume a building is worth $2 million. The insured purchases an insurance policy worth $1 million with a $10,000 deductible. The reimbursement amount will not exceed 50% ($1 million / $2 million) of the value of the loss minus the deductible ($10,000). Consequently, if a covered loss is valued at $500,000, the policy will reimburse $240,000.

$$\$500,000 \times 0.50 = \$250,000$$

$$\$250,000 - \$10,000 = \$240,000$$

The **builder's risk reporting form** gradually raises the insurance amount on a building under construction. As the building increases in value, the coverage amount also increases.

CONDOMINIUM COVERAGE FORMS

Condominium coverage forms are divided into two types:

- **Condominium association coverage forms** – These apply to residential or commercial condominium associations, and insure the following items against direct physical loss or damage: buildings (including permanently attached fixtures and machinery and certain personal property); business personal property (owned by the insured or individual unit-owners); others' personal property that is in the insured's care.
- **Condominium commercial unit-owners coverage forms** – These apply only to commercial condominium owners, and insure the following items against direct physical loss or damage: personal property owned by the unit-owner and other's personal property that is in the insured's care.

The cause of loss form lists the specific perils insured by condominium coverage. If damage occurs to a property covered by both association and unit-owner forms, the association form takes precedence.

WORKERS COMPENSATION AND EMPLOYERS LIABILITY POLICY

Workers compensation and employer's liability policy is used by private insurance companies to provide workers' compensation coverage on behalf of employers. It consists of seven sections: general section, part one—workers compensation, part two—employer's liability, part three—other state insurance, part four—your duties of injury occurs, part five—premium, and part six—conditions. **General section** includes policy definitions and conditions.

Part one—workers compensation reimburses any benefits or compensation the insured is obligated to pay under state workers' compensation laws. There is no dollar limit, and the injury must have been sustained over the policy period.

Part two—employers liability applies when the insured is liable under common law to pay expenses resulting from work-related injuries or occupational diseases. This coverage reimburses a minimum of $100,000 per accident and a separate minimum limit per employee for occupational disease.

Part two—employers liability excludes losses when they result from the following:

- Punitive damages incurred while a worker was illegally employed
- Violation of state and federal law
- Injuries to illegally-employed workers when the insured was aware of the illegal employment
- Damages awarded under various federal laws
- Liability assumed under contract
- Injury to a vessel's crew or master
- Damages incurred by violating discrimination, harassment, and other employment practice laws
- Injuries outside the coverage territory, unless worker was only temporarily outside the area
- Injuries that the insured intentionally causes
- Injuries already assumed under federal workers' compensation laws
- Obligations the insured must fulfill under workers' compensation laws, disability laws, and other applicable laws

Part three—other states insurance section provides workers' compensation coverage in states that are not identified in the information page on part one, but may obligate the employer to provide such coverage via a private insurer. The insured will not receive coverage unless he notifies the insurance company of when he intends to start work in the new state.

Part four—your duties if injury occurs section explains the insured's obligations in the event of a covered injury. These duties include the following: paying the injury party's medical expenses, notifying the insurance company of the injury, and helping the insurer as it investigates and settles the claim.

Part five—premium section lays out the method for figuring policy cost.

Part six—conditions section explains cancellation procedures, the insurer's right to inspect the insured's workplace, and other policy conditions.

COMMERCIAL CRIME INSURANCE

Commercial crime insurance insures businesses and government entities against theft, robbery, employee dishonesty, and similar crimes. It can be acquired as either a mono-line policy (known as a policy form) or as part of a commercial package policy (known as a coverage form). Standard mono-line policies for commercial crime insurance include the following:

- Commercial crime policy—discovery version
- Commercial crime policy—loss sustained version
- Government crime policy—discovery version
- Government crime policy—loss sustained version

Standard package policy forms for commercial crime insurance include the following:

- Commercial crime coverage form—discovery version
- Commercial crime coverage form —loss sustained version
- Government crime coverage form —discovery version
- Government crime coverage form —loss sustained version

Each type of commercial crime insurance form (commercial/government or policy/coverage) can be divided into two versions: **discovery** and **loss sustained**.

Theft involves unlawfully removing money, securities, or property by force or by stealth, and includes burglary, safe burglary, and robbery.

Burglary occurs when a person unlawfully enters or leaves the premises and removes property that was inside the premises. It can only be proven by finding evidence of forced entry or exit.

Safe burglary occurs when a person unlawfully enters a locked safe or vault and removes property, or unlawfully removes the entire safe or vault from the premises. Again, there must be evidence of forced entry via marks on the safe or vault.

Robbery occurs when one person unlawfully takes property in another person's possession. The act must have involved some threat of bodily harm to the person who was allegedly robbed, or some blatantly unlawful act to which the victim is witness.

Forgery involves unlawfully signing the name of another person or organization.

COVERAGES ON COMMERCIAL CRIME INSURANCE

Forgery or alteration coverage reimburses losses that result when checks, drafts, promissory notes, and similar documents are forged or altered in the name of the named insured or his agent. Coverage applies worldwide and in situations in which fake signatures have been mechanically created. Additionally, the insurance company may pay the insured's court costs if he is sued for not paying for forged or altered documents.

Inside the premises—theft of money and securities coverage provides theft, disappearance, and destruction coverage for money and securities stored within the insured's premises. It also covers the interior or exterior of the premises, locked safes, vaults, cash registers, cash drawers, and cash boxes if they are damaged during theft or forced entry.

Inside the premises—robbery or safe burglary of other property covers **other property** (any property that is not money or securities) when it is lost in the following situations: robbery or attempted robbery of a custodian inside the premises, or safe burglary or attempted safe burglary of a safe or vault inside the premises. This coverage also reimburses the following: damage to the premises' exterior or interior if the insured is liable and damage to locked safes and vaults if they are contained within the premises and the damage results from actual or attempted robbery/safe burglary.

Computer fraud coverage applies when a computer is used to illegally transfer money, securities, or other property from inside the premises to a location beyond the premises. It provides worldwide coverage against loss or damage.

Outside the premises coverage reimburses the following losses:

- Money and securities that are stolen, lost, or destroyed outside the premises, if they are in the possession of a messenger or armored car company
- Other property that is lost outside the premises during an actual or attempted robbery, if the property is in the possession of a messenger or armored car company

Money orders and counterfeit paper currency coverage reimburses the insured when he takes counterfeit currency or invalid money orders in good faith as payment.

Funds transfer fraud coverage reimburses the insured when he loses money from a transfer account because a financial institution has received fraudulent instructions from a person who is impersonating the insured or his employees without the insured's knowledge or consent. Transfer accounts allow the insured to electronically transfer funds via phone or written request. This coverage does not apply to property that is lost because of fraudulent transfers through a computer.

Extortion—commercial entities endorsement coverage reimburses any money, securities, or other property that is lost due to **extortion**, which occurs when a person obtains property from the insured by threatening him, his employees, his relatives, or his employees' relatives with bodily harm. The person must be holding the relatives captive.

Employee theft coverage applies whenever an employee steals company property, even if the employee is never identified, and reimburses loss of money, securities, and other types of property. This coverage does not apply in the following situations:

- An employee cancels and does not reinstate similar insurance.
- Warehouse receipts are used in a fraudulent and dishonest manner.
- Someone trades in the insured's name or with a fictitious account.
- The only evidence of loss is inventory shortage or profit and loss calculations.

Losses can be reimbursed on a **per loss basis**, which pays out the maximum insurance limit without regard to the number of employees involved, or a **per employee basis**, which pays all losses for a single employee.

EXCLUSIONS ON COMMERCIAL CRIME INSURANCE

Commercial crime insurance excludes losses from coverage if they result from the following:

- Nuclear dangers
- War or war-like actions
- Indirect and consequential events
- Government authority seizing or destroying property
- Theft /dishonest acts when they involve the insured, partners, members, employees, directors, trustees, or authorized representatives, unless they are covered under employee theft coverage (This exclusion applies regardless of whether or not these people are acting alone or in collusion with others.)

Computer fraud excludes losses from coverage if they result from the following:

- Giving away too much property as part of a business transaction or exchange
- Funds transfer fraud
- The insured or someone working for the insured voluntarily parting with property because he has been deceived into doing so

Inside the premises—theft of money and security, inside the premises—robbery or safe burglary of other property and outside the premises coverages excludes losses if they result from the following:

- Accounting/arithmetic errors and omissions
- Giving away too much property as part of a business transaction
- Named insured or representatives of the name insured voluntarily parting with property because he/they has been deceived into doing so
- Fire damage, unless it involves safes, vaults, money, or securities
- Malfunctions in money-operated devices, expect for instances in which the device has recording equipment
- Damage to motor vehicles, trailers, or semitrailers
- Malicious mischief or vandalism causing damage to the insured premises' interior or exterior, safes, vaults, cash registers, cash drawers, and other property
- Unauthorized instructions causing the transference or surrendering of property outside the premises, unless the property was outside the premises and in the possession of a messenger

CONDITIONS ON COMMERCIAL CRIME INSURANCE

The **consolidation or merger** condition provides automatic coverage for employees and premises acquired due to a merger or consolidation. Coverage only lasts 90 days, and is not available for government entities. The **limit of insurance** condition prevents the insurance limit from accumulating throughout the lifetime of the policy.

According to the **insured's duties in the event of a loss** condition, the insured has the following responsibilities when a loss occurs:

- Alert the insurance company of the loss
- Alert the proper authorities if a crime has been committed
- Provide sworn testimony if the insurer requests it
- Submit a sworn proof of loss within 120 days following the loss
- Help the insurer investigate and settle the claim

Under the **other insurance** condition, crime insurance policies provide reimbursement on an excess basis if more than one policy is covering the same loss.

The **employee theft coverage** condition provides coverage for employees who are outside the coverage area, provided they have not been out of the coverage area for longer than 90 days.

According to the **forgery or alteration coverage** condition, following a loss, the insured must produce either the instrument that is part of the loss or an affidavit describing the loss.

Inside the premises—robbery or safe burglary of other property coverage and **outside the premises coverage** conditions apply a $5,000 limit on each occurrence in which precious metals, fur, pearls, or precious/semiprecious stones are lost.

According to the **outside the premises coverage** condition, the insurance company is only obligated to reimburse the amount not paid by the armored car company.

Computer fraud coverage condition applies a $5,000 limit on each occurrence in which manuscripts, drawings, or records are damaged.

LOSS SUSTAINED FORM

Under a **loss sustained form**, losses are covered if they are sustained or discovered during the policy period, or if they are discovered within a year of the policy's expiration date. Once the insured obtains a new commercial crime insurance policy, the yearlong discovery period ends. According to the **loss sustained during prior insurance condition**, these forms will pay back losses that were discovered during the current policy period, even if they were sustained during the previous policy period. This condition does not apply unless three criteria are present:

- The previous policy's discovery period has ended
- The current policy's effective date was the same day as the previous policy's expiration date
- Both the current and the previous policy cover the loss

DISCOVERY FORM

Discovery forms cover any losses, no matter when they occurred, as long as they are discovered during the policy period or within 60 days of the policy's expiration date. This 60-day period is extended to one year for losses resulting from employee benefit plans. The discovery period ends as soon as a new commercial crime insurance policy is acquired. To discover a loss, the insured must know of a past loss or an impending loss (though he is not required to know the exact amount of the loss or its details), and he must receive an actual or potential claim of a covered loss. Commercial crime insurance offers the following coverages via agreement or endorsement: employee theft, forgery/alteration, computer fraud, outside the premises, inside the premises—theft of money and securities, inside the premises—robbery or safe burglary of other property, funds transfer fraud, and money orders and counterfeit paper currency.

EQUIPMENT BREAKDOWN COVERAGE

Equipment breakdown coverage (also called **boiler and machinery coverage**) covers business equipment against property damage, provided the damage is caused by **breakdown**, which is limited to pressure or vacuum equipment failure, mechanical failure, and electrical failure. The following types of equipment are covered:

- Equipment designed to work under internal pressure
- Energy transmitting equipment that is electrical or mechanical in nature
- Equipment designed to provide a utility service for the insured, provided the equipment is owned by the utility company
- Computers and communication equipment

Equipment breakdown coverage reimburses direct loss, including damage to business equipment, and indirect loss, including costs that are incurred due to business interruption. This coverage can be acquired as a mono-line policy or as part of a commercial package policy with the following sections: **commercial package policy declarations, commercial package policy common conditions, equipment breakdown protection coverage form, equipment breakdown protection coverage declarations, and endorsements.**

Equipment breakdown protection coverage forms will not pay more than the following sublimits for the corresponding losses:

- $25,000 for expediting expenses
- $25,000 for hazardous substance limitation
- $25,000 for ammonia contamination
- $25,000 for water damage limitation

In most cases, $250 is the minimum deductible on these forms. According to the **actual cash value endorsement**, property damage caused by breakdown is reimbursed at the lesser of the following values: actual cash value of damaged property, or repair or replacement cost of damaged property. According to the **business income—report of values endorsement**, sales earnings, profits, and value projections over a 12-month period must be reported. Equipment breakdown protection coverage forms provide the following coverages (as long as the cause of loss is breakdown):

- **Property damage** – This reimburses direct damage.
- **Expediting expenses** – This pays for the cost of replacing or repairing (either permanently or temporarily) damage.
- **Business income and extra expense** – This can also apply to locations that the insured neither owns nor operates.
- **Spoilage damage** – This reimburses damage to raw materials, manufactured products, and products in storage.
- **Utility interruption** – This covers damage caused by breakdown of utility equipment the insured does not own.
- **Automatic coverage for newly acquired property** – This covers equipment breakdowns at new locations for 90 days, provided the insurance company is notified of the acquisition.
- **Ordinance or law** – This is covered if the cause of loss is breakdown.
- **Brands and labels** – This helps to salvage damaged property.
- **Error or omissions** – This covers losses resulting from accidental omissions in the policy's declaration sections, failures to list all premises owned by the insured within the policy, and omissions that cause cancellation of coverage.

Equipment breakdown protection coverage forms generally exclude losses that are both accidental and indirect in nature, including losses resulting from the following:

- Ordinance or law
- War acts
- Nuclear hazards
- Earthquake
- Natural wear and tear
- Business activity interruption
- Combustion explosion
- Equipment that is outdated or improperly maintained
- Insufficient power, light, steam, heating, or cooling
- Water damage caused by fire extinguishing systems
- Damage to an object during testing

Defense condition obligates the insurer to either settle or defend a lawsuit in which the insured may be liable for damage to others' property in his care.

According to the **valuation condition**, property damage is valued at the cost of repair, replacement, or building.

According to the **reducing your loss condition**, the insured must minimize his loss following a breakdown and restore business operations as soon as possible.

Privilege to adjust with owner condition empowers the insurer to settle liability suits with the property owner.

The **suspension condition** empowers the insurer to suspend coverage when equipment has been placed in an inherently dangerous situation. Although the insurer is not obligated to provide advance warning, it must send notification of the suspension to the address of the insured or the equipment.

According to the **final settlement between insurers condition**, when more than one insurer is trying to settle a disputed or arbitrated loss, the insurer with the greater loss obligation must repay the other insurers' excess contributions.

The **joint or disputed loss agreement condition** applies when the same loss is covered by two different insurers (a commercial property policy and an equipment breakdown protection policy), and they cannot agree on their respective reimbursement obligations. In most cases, both insurers will reimburse the full amount of any loss that is indisputably covered under their own policies and half the amount of any disputed loss.

OCCURRENCE FORMS AND CLAIMS-MADE FORMS

Commercial general liability insurance uses two basic coverage forms: occurrence forms and claims-made forms. Under **occurrence forms**, coverage applies to any covered loss occurring within the policy territory and during the policy period. If a claim on a loss is not filed until after the policy has expired, the loss is still covered, as long as it occurred during the policy period. Under **claims-made forms**, coverage applies to any claim filed during the policy period. In essence, even a covered loss occurring outside the policy period can receive coverage, as long as the claim was filed during the policy period. Claims-made forms often include a **retroactive date**, which protects the insurer against excessive risk. If a covered loss occurs prior to this date, the insurer is not obligated to cover it. In most cases, the insured can select a retroactive date from three available options: the policy-effective date, a date earlier than the policy-effective date, or no retroactive date.

RULES GOVERNING THE CHANGING OF RETROACTIVE DATES ON CLAIMS-MADE FORMS

Changing or advancing retroactive dates on claims-made forms can create coverage gaps, which leave the insured without coverage for a period of time. These should be avoided whenever possible. Therefore, when acquiring a new claims-made policy, the insured should make certain that the retroactive date on the new policy is identical to the old policy. Furthermore, retroactive dates cannot be advanced unless the insured provides written consent and one of the following criteria is present:

- A new policy is written by a different insurance company
- The insured failed to provide the necessary material information, or omitted material information that would have affected the insurance company's decision to provide insurance
- The insured's business has undergone a change that increases the insurer's risk exposure

EXTENDED REPORTING PERIOD

Extended reporting periods are available for claims-made forms. They help eliminate coverage gaps by covering claims submitted after the policy has expired. Extended reporting periods are available only under the following conditions:

- The insured cancels or does not renew his claims-made form
- The insured replaces the claims-made form with an occurrence form
- The insurance company renews or replaces the current form with a form that lists an earlier retroactive date

Depending on policy conditions, forms may provide extended reporting periods of 60 days or 5 years at no extra charge or additional premiums to the insured. During the 60-day period, the insurance company will cover any valid claim, as long as the loss occurred between the policy's retroactive date and the expiration date. In some cases, the insured may know of a situation that would cause him to receive claims after the 60-day period has elapsed. If the insured alerts the insurance company of his situation within the 60 days, he can receive an extended reporting period of five years for claims related to that situation.

FIDELITY BONDS

Name schedule bonds provide a certain amount of coverage for every employee scheduled on the policy. Each employee may have a different coverage amount.

Position schedule bonds provide a certain amount of coverage for each position scheduled on the policy rather than each employee. When a new employee is hired, he will immediately receive the coverage inherent to his position.

Commercial blanket bonds reimburse losses the insured may incur when an employee or employees commit dishonest acts. The limit of liability applies on a per occurrence basis, regardless of the number of employees involved in that occurrence. No specific employees or positions are named in the policy.

Blanket position bonds provide coverage against dishonest acts committed by employees. However, reimbursement is made on a per employee basis rather than a per occurrence basis.

WORKERS' COMPENSATION INSURANCE

Workers' compensation insurance applies to employees who have been injured during the course of their job activities. It covers the following costs:

- **Medical expenses** – This covers any reasonable medical costs for the insured.
- **Rehabilitation benefits** – This pays for physical therapy and vocational rehabilitation.
- **Disability/loss of income benefits** – This provides loss of income reimbursement when employees are unable to work.
- **Survivor/death benefits** – These are paid out to surviving dependents if the insured dies.

Under **workers' compensation laws**, employers are obligated to pay most expenses when employees are injured at work or suffer from occupational diseases, no matter who was at fault. Consequently, these laws provide the only available benefits, known as the **exclusive remedy**, for injured workers. They cannot sue their employers for additional benefits. Most employees in the country are covered by workers' compensation, except for the following exempt classes: specific types of farm and agricultural workers, charitable organization workers, newspaper vendors, and domestic employees and casual laborers.

There are four levels of disability under workers' compensation: **permanent total, permanent partial, temporary total,** and **temporary partial. Permanent disabilities** persist for the remainder of the worker's lifetime. **Temporary disabilities** will heal completely at some point. The definitions of **total** and **partial** depend on whether the state abides by the **industrial disability** standard or the **medical disability** standard. Under the industrial disability standard, a total injury means the worker no longer has any ability to work, while a partial injury means the worker can earn some income by working. Under the medical disability standard, a total injury means the worker has lost any physical functioning, while a partial injury means the worker retains partial physical functioning. If an injury is partial, a worker can no longer perform his current job, but may be able to perform another, lower paying job. Therefore, workers' compensation would reimburse the income difference between his old job and his new job. If the injury is total, a worker can no longer perform any job. Therefore, workers' compensation would reimburse his entire income.

COMPULSORY LAWS, ELECTIVE LAWS, AND COMPENSABLE INJURIES

Depending on the state, workers' compensation laws can be compulsory or elective. In **compulsory** states, employers are obligated to abide by all workers' compensation laws. In **elective** states, employers have the option of abiding or not abiding by workers' compensation laws. If they choose not to abide by these laws, however, they sacrifice certain incentives, such as common law defense and caps on their liability exposures in the event of worker injury. For certain types of occupations (i.e. government employees), workers' compensation laws are always compulsory, regardless of the state in which the worker lives.

Workers' compensation laws only cover **compensable injuries**, which are injuries that arise out of employment or in the course of employment.

AVIATION INSURANCE

Aviation insurance includes two basic coverages: aircraft hull insurance and aircraft liability insurance. **Aircraft hull insurance** covers physical damage to the aircraft, airframe, engines, controls, and electronic equipment related to navigation and communications. Coverage is available in these situations:

- The aircraft is in the air or on the ground.
- The aircraft is on the ground only.
- The aircraft is being towed by a separate vehicle.

Aircraft liability insurance covers the following: bodily injuries to passengers as well as people who are not passengers, property damage liability, and medical expenses resulting from passengers who sustain injuries.

UMBRELLA LIABILITY INSURANCE

Umbrella liability insurance provides excess liability coverage (often millions of dollars) over the regular limit of an existing, or underlying, policy, and can cover perils not included under the existing policy. Umbrella policies go into effect once the original limit is exhausted or the insured suffers a loss not covered by the underlying policy. Umbrella insurance can apply on a personal basis, providing additional liability coverage on homeowner's and auto policies, or a commercial basis, expanding coverage on commercial general liability policies. The insured is not required to pay a deductible, but if the underlying policy expires prior to the occurrence of a covered loss, the insured will have to pay the original limit of insurance out of pocket before the umbrella policy will

go into effect. Because umbrella policies cover many types of liability losses, they are not considered indemnity contracts.

Casualty Insurance Terms and Related Concepts

INSURANCE

Insurance is one method of transferring risk. Organizations purchase insurance contracts from third parties, who assume responsibility for any loss or liability associated with a particular risk event if it occurs. Fire insurance, for example, covers any losses caused by fire damage. In most cases, an insurance company charges a premium for its services and distributes damage payments from the combined premiums collected from all organizations. In order to calculate premiums, loss ratios, and other insurance information for a specific policy, the insurance company must collect risk data from a group of similar items. For instance, when determining the theft insurance premium for a particular home, an insurance company calculates the total number of thefts in a population of similar homes. According to the **law of large numbers**, larger populations allow for more accurate calculations, while smaller populations result in less accurate calculations.

CASUALTY INSURANCE

People and businesses purchase **casualty insurance** to protect themselves against liabilities and to reimburse the cost of paying legal settlements. Specifically, casualty insurance protects against **civil wrongs**, also known as **torts**, which involve the private (non-contractual) relationships between parties. There are two types of torts coverable by casualty insurance:

- Bodily or personal injury to another person that results from the insured's alleged failure to take proper care
- Damage to another person's personal property that results from the insured's alleged failure to take proper care

Casualty insurance does not protect against **criminal acts**, which are prosecuted by authorities at the state and federal level. A person or business convicted of a criminal act may pay fines that are not covered by insurance.

CERTIFICATE OF INSURANCE, REPRESENTATIONS, AND WARRANTIES

A **certificate of insurance** indicates that a policy has been written and issued. It can serve as evidence of coverage when various legal and financial issues arise. If the insurance covers a group of people, one person will be designated as the **certificate holder**.

Representations are statements provided by the applicant that are true to the best of his knowledge. Representations make up most of the information on an application. However, insurance companies cannot void the application based on representations because they are not contractual matters.

Warranties are agreements between the insured party and the insurance provider, and are part of the insurance policy. If a warranty is violated either purposefully or accidentally, the entire policy can be voided.

RISK

Risk is the likelihood that an organization will incur some type of loss. It only applies to uncertain and unpredictable events, such as theft, accidental damage, or weather damage. Organizations can handle risk using a variety of strategies:

- **Avoidance** – The risk is avoided. For instance, an organization can avoid earthquake damage simply by not building near fault lines.
- **Reduction** – The loss associated with the risk is reduced. A possible reduction strategy would be installing a security fence in an effort to reduce the number of burglary attempts.
- **Transference** – The responsibility for a risk is transferred to a third party. One type of transference strategy is acquiring insurance, such as a **hold harmless agreement**, in which a contractor agrees to accept responsibility and liability if a particular risk event should occur.
- **Retention (or acceptance)** – An organization does nothing to mitigate the risk. It simply accepts any consequences, losses, or liabilities associated with a particular risk event.

Not all risks are insurable. In most cases, a person or organization cannot acquire insurance for a risk unless the following criteria are present:

- The person or organization must have an **insurable interest** in the risk.
- The risk must be **pure**, not **speculative**.
- The risk must be accidental and unexpected.
- For the purpose of setting a policy period, the risk must be constrained to a definite place and time.
- The risk must involve substantial loss.
- The loss from the risk must result in financial hardship for the person or organization.
- The insurance company must be able to calculate any loss incurred as a result of the risk event.
- The person or organization must be able to afford the insurance premiums.
- The law of large numbers must apply. Otherwise, the insurance company will not be able to calculate premiums due to a lack of cases.

INSURABLE INTEREST, PURE RISK, AND SPECULATIVE RISK

An **insurable interest** must be present before insurance can be acquired. A person or organization only possesses an insurable interest if they stand to lose money when the insured item (person or property) is damaged. For instance, a person has an insurable interest in his own life or property, but not the life or property of another individual. Therefore, he cannot purchase life or property insurance on another individual.

A **speculative risk** is any risk that offers an opportunity for both gain and loss. Speculative risks are **not coverable** by insurance. An example of a speculative risk is a stock market investment.

A **pure risk** is any risk that presents only the opportunity for loss, and is the only type of risk covered by insurance. Examples of pure risks include theft and fire.

NEGLIGENCE

Negligence is an **unintentional tort**, and is caused by the insured's accidental failure to exercise reasonable care to prevent injury or damages. In most cases, casualty insurance does not cover

intentional torts. The insured cannot be held liable for damages unless the accuser can prove negligence, which requires establishing the presence of four factors:

- A legal duty must be owed. The insured is legally obligated to act in a **reasonable** and **prudent** manner to protect the safety and property of another person.
- The legal duty owed must have been breached. The insured may owe different levels of protection to different people. These different levels are known as a **degree** or **standard of care**.
- The insured's failure to act must have been the **proximate cause** of the act.
- There must be an actual injury or property damage.

According to the **contributory negligence** law, if a person has sustained damages or injury through some fault of his own, he cannot hold another party liable, even if they share responsibility for those damages.

According to the **comparative negligence** law, if a person has sustained damages or injury due to his own fault and the fault of a separate party, the court will assess and award damages based on the level of responsibility held by each party. Consider, for instance, a person who is injured while shopping at a store. The court may rule that the person is 20% responsible for his injuries and the store is 80% responsible. Consequently, the person would receive 80% of the possible damage settlement.

People and organizations can use the following defenses against accusations of negligence:

- **Assumption of risk** – The injured party has no right to collect damages if he knew the risks beforehand and still placed himself in the situation.
- **Intervening cause** – The accused is not liable if the damage or injury was caused by an intervening cause beyond his control.
- **Last clear chance defense** – The injured party has no right to collect damages if he had the **last clear chance** to circumvent the loss and ignored it.
- **Contributory negligence** – The injured party cannot hold another party liable if his injuries were partly his own fault.
- **Comparative negligence** – The injured party is only entitled to part of the damages if he was partly responsible for his injuries.

If a party is found liable, it may have to pay the following damages: **punitive** and/or **compensatory**, which includes **special damages** (fixed expenses such as medical bills) and **general damages** (non-economic expenses such as pain and suffering).

PRINCIPLE OF INDEMNITY AND ALEATORY CONTRACT

The **principle of indemnity** applies when the insurance contract begins issuing payments following a loss. It dictates that the insured must be returned to his or her approximate financial state before the loss occurred. Indemnity does not always cover the actual loss amount. For instance, valued or stated amount policies may issue payments totaling more than the actual loss amount, while deductible or coinsurance policies may pay out less than the total loss.

An **aleatory** contract is one in which the exchange of value between the two parties may be unequal. Insurance contracts are aleatory because their payout is based on the occurrence of an uncertain event. If the event never occurs, the insured party never receives any goods or services in exchange for their premium payments. If the event does occur, the insurance company may pay out more than it has received in premiums.

112

Sources Used by Underwriters to Determine the Risk Level Posed by Insurance Applicants

When determining whether or not an applicant should be insured, underwriters assess the applicant's risk level by examining the following sources: the application, the company's claim files, industry bureaus, government agencies, inspections services, other insurers, and financial information services. Because many of these sources provide highly personal information, underwriters must abide by the **Fair Credit Reporting Act**. Underwriters must be wary of **adverse selection**, which applies to applicants who are especially susceptible to a certain kind of loss. A person living in Kansas, for instance, might face a high risk of storm damage. Consequently, an insurance company could face substantial losses if it provided storm insurance for a large number of individuals living in Kansas.

State Insurance Department's Responsibilities Regarding the Approval of New Rates and Forms

When an insurance company changes its rates or policy forms, it requires approval from the insurance department in its state of operation. Different states have unique ways of granting approval:

- **Prior approval states** – These must approve the new rate or form before the insurance company can use it.
- **File and use states** – These allow companies to use new rates and forms immediately after they have been filed, and filing must occur within a certain time period after first use. The insurance department will accept or reject the changes at a later date.
- **Mandatory states** – These require companies to use forms and rates that are standard in that state.
- **Open competition states** – These permit companies to use the rates they select and compete with them. However, they still must abide by nondiscrimination and adequacy regulations.

Casualty Policy Provisions

DEDUCTIBLE AND SUBROGATION

At the beginning of a contract, the insured may pay a **deductible**, which reduces the monthly premium payment. The deductible amount equals part of the potential loss, but does not decrease the amount of insurance coverage. Higher deductibles create lower premium payments, but may prove unprofitable for smaller losses. The declaration section lists the exact deductible amount.

Subrogation rights empower the insurer to seek compensation from a third party if they were responsible for the loss. In effect, if the insured suffers a loss due to the activities of another person, the insurance company can reimburse the loss and then sue the responsible person in order to recover damages. Many policies include subrogation conditions, also known as **Transfer of Right of Recovery Against Others to Us**, which transfers the **right of recovery** from the insured to the insurer.

SUPPLEMENTARY COSTS

Supplementary costs are any costs covered by liability insurance, **except** damages and injuries. They are paid on top of the regular liability limit of the policy, and normally include the following:

- Defense costs
- First aid rendered to people during and immediately after the accident
- Costs resulting from claim investigation
- Bond premium payments, including appeal bonds, attachment bonds, bail bonds, etc.
- Any reasonable costs resulting from a request by the insurance company to investigate or defend claims
- Loss of earnings – In many cases, the insured loses income because he has to miss work or leave early to appear in court
- Prejudgment interest, if it is not listed as a damage under the insuring agreements section
- Post judgment interest

Defense costs include the expenses of defending the insured against liability lawsuits, including lawsuits that are completely baseless. Liability insurance pays for defense costs in addition to the regular liability limit of the policy. However, the policy will cease to pay defense costs once it has reimbursed damages up to its limits.

Prejudgment interest is the amount in damages the injured party would have earned if he had started receiving payments immediately after the injury. In many cases, courts award prejudgment interest to the injured. Policies generally cover prejudgment interest either by including it as part of the insuring agreement or by making additional payments.

Post judgment interest is the amount that accrues between the time the damage settlement is awarded and the time the company begins issuing payments.

SUPPLEMENTARY PAYMENTS AVAILABLE ON COVERAGES A AND B OF COMMERCIAL GENERAL LIABILITY INSURANCE

Coverages A and B offer the following supplementary payments in addition to the limits of insurance:

- $250 maximum for bail bonds
- Any expenses the insurance company sustains
- Indemnitee defense costs
- Interest on prejudgment and postjudgment rulings
- Expenses the insured may incur as a result of taxes levied in a suit
- Expenses the insured has to pay in his efforts to help investigate and defend a claim (includes a $250 per day maximum for lost earnings)
- Bond expenses to release attachments

The policy will cover the defense costs of a third party if his damages are caused by a covered loss. Third party coverage is not considered a supplementary payment because it deducts from the limits of insurance. If the insured and indemnitee are named in the same lawsuit, however, and the insured's liability is covered by the policy, the indemnitee's defense costs will be included under supplementary payments, and will not deduct from the limits of insurance.

CONDITIONS ON COMMERCIAL GENERAL LIABILITY POLICIES

The insured has the following **duties in the event of occurrence, offense, claim, or suit**:

- Notify the insurer promptly of all pertinent information related to an occurrence or offense that may bring about a claim.
- Record and provide written notice of claim specifics (date, etc.) to the insured promptly following the making of a claim or suit.
- Facilitate the insurer's efforts to gather records.
- Make certain the insurer receives all demands, notices, and applicable legal papers in a prompt manner.
- Help the insurer pursue parties that are liable to the insured.
- Help the insurer investigate, settle, and defend claims.
- Do not agree to any payment or obligation, except rendering first aid, unless the insurer consents to such an agreement.

The **when we do not renew condition** places certain requirements on the insurance company when it decides against renewing a policy. It must provide the insured with written notification at least 30 days before the policy's expiration date.

CONDITIONS ON COMMERCIAL CRIME INSURANCE

Under the **cancellation as to any employee condition**, an employee's coverage is terminated as soon as the named insured or partners, directors, officers, members, or managers discover the employee has committed theft or another dishonest act, regardless of whether the act occurred before or after the employee was hired. The insurance company can also cancel employee coverage, provided it gives written notification to the insured at least 30 days before the effective cancellation date.

The **valuation condition** mandates the following:

- When money is lost, the loss is reimbursed at face value.
- When securities are lost, the loss is reimbursed at the security's face value on the close of business on the day the damage occurred.
- When other property is damaged, the loss is reimbursed using one of the following methods: replacement cost of the property, repair/replacement cost of the property, or the limit of insurance—whichever is smaller.

LIMIT OF LIABILITY AND SUPPLEMENTARY PAYMENTS AVAILABLE UNDER PART A OF AN AUTO POLICY

The limit of liability on Part A is provided on either a **single limit basis** or a **split limit basis**. Under a single limit, bodily injury and property damage are covered collectively with a single amount, such as $75,000. Under a split limit, each type of liability has a separate limit. Split limits are expressed as a sequence of three numbers, such as 20/40/15:

- $20,000 for bodily injury per person
- $40,000 for bodily injury per accident
- $15,000 for property damage per accident

Part A makes the following supplementary payments, which are made in addition to the limits of liability:

- Appeal bond premiums
- Release attachment bond premiums
- $250 maximum on bail bonds
- Post judgment interest
- $200 per day maximum to reimburse losses in earnings due to hearing and trial appearances
- Any reasonable additional expenses the insured must pay at the company's request

EXCLUSIONS UNDER PART A, B, AND C OF AN AUTO POLICY

Part A excludes the following liabilities from coverage:

- Bodily injury or property damage that the insured has purposefully caused
- Bodily injury or property damage that is already covered by a Nuclear Energy Liability policy
- Bodily injury sustained by an employee of the insured
- Property damage that occurs when the insured is renting or using the property
- Property damage that occurs when the insured owns or is transporting the property
- Damage to off-road vehicles and vehicles with less than four wheels
- Liability incurred when the insured's auto is involved in an auto business
- Liability incurred when a vehicle is being used without the insured's permission
- Liability incurred when a vehicle is a contestant in a prearranged race
- Liability incurred when a vehicle is not a covered auto owned or used by family members

Part B excludes injuries from coverage if they result from the following:

- Occupying a motor vehicle that has less than four wheels
- Participating in a prearranged race or contest

116

- Using a covered auto as a means of public or livery transportation
- Using the vehicle as part of the insured's business
- Occupying a vehicle that is also used as a residence
- Occupying a vehicle that is uninsured, even when the insured owns it
- Another person occupying an uninsured vehicle that is owned or regularly used by the insured's family member
- An insured occupying a vehicle when he does not have permission or reasonable evidence of entitlement to do so
- War or nuclear hazards
- Accidents already covered by worker's compensation

Part C excludes the following losses from coverage:

- Bodily injury to the insured when he is occupying or struck by an auto that is owned by the insured but not covered under the policy's Uninsured Motorist Coverage
- Bodily injury to a family member of the insured when he is occupying or struck by an auto that is owned by the insured and covered by another policy
- Damage to an auto being used for livery or public transportation
- Settlements made without permission from the insured
- Damage involving an auto that the insured is using without entitlement or permission to do so

Property and Casualty Practice Test

1. HO-2, HO-3, HO-4, HO-5, HO-6, and HO-8 are all types of homeowners policies. Which two sets of policies are not solely designed for owner-occupied dwellings?

    a. HO-2 and HO-8
    b. HO-4 and HO-6
    c. HO-3 and HO-4
    d. HO-5 and HO-8

2. The HO-8, also known as the modified coverage form, is designed to meet the needs of what type of insured?

    a. Subsidized housing owners.
    b. Owners of seasonal rental locations where the value of the dwelling exceeds the replacement cost value.
    c. Owners of a historic home whose replacement cost value exceeds the value of the home itself.
    d. Tenant-occupied locations in a poor protection class area.

3. A tenant who does not need to buy coverage for the dwelling itself but would like to cover his own personal property should obtain which type of homeowners policy?

    a. HO-4
    b. HO-2
    c. HO-5
    d. HO-6

4. To obtain the broadest coverage available for an owner-occupied dwelling, the insured should purchase which type of homeowner's policy?

    a. HO-5 comprehensive form
    b. HO-2 broad form
    c. HO-6 unit-owners form
    d. HO-8 modified coverage form

5. Broad form provides coverage for which of the following perils?

    a. Theft
    b. Glass breakage
    c. Smoke
    d. Riot

6. An unendorsed DP-3 policy does not provide coverage for which of the following exposures?

    a. Garages
    b. Storage sheds
    c. Debris removal
    d. Theft

7. The DP-3 Dwelling Form contains all of the following coverages EXCEPT:

    a. Coverage A – Land
    b. Coverage B – Other Structures
    c. Coverage C – Personal Property
    d. Coverage D – Fair Rental Value

8. Special forms coverage is coverage on a DP policy form that combines broad form perils with what other form of perils?

    a. Basic form perils
    b. Open perils
    c. Special perils
    d. Modified perils

9. Coverage C – Personal Property provides coverage for the insured's personal property under what circumstance?

    a. While in the possession of the insured
    b. While on the covered premises
    c. Worldwide coverage
    d. When the insured knowingly loans the property to a family member off premises

10. Risks can be classified as pure or speculative. Which of the two, pure or speculative, is always undesirable from an investor's point of view?

    a. Speculative
    b. Speculative and pure
    c. Pure
    d. Neither

11. Which hazard is defined as intentionally causing, fabricating, or exaggerating a loss?

    a. Moral hazard
    b. Morale hazard
    c. Physical hazard
    d. Legal hazard

12. There are four types of hazards that cause a loss. An insured failing to salt and shovel her sidewalk after a snowstorm presents what type of hazard?

    a. Morale hazard
    b. Moral hazard
    c. Legal hazard
    d. Physical hazard

13. Sara is the owner of a gift shop that was struggling to make enough money to cover its bills. Sara knew there were reports of robberies in the area but continued to leave the doors to the store unlocked after she would leave at night. Sara figured if her store was robbed she could collect the insurance money and pay off some debt. Sara's carelessness is an example of what type of hazard?

    a. Moral hazard
    b. Morale hazard
    c. Physical hazard
    d. Legal hazard

14. There are three elements to a loss exposure. What can be defined as a cause of loss?

a. Peril
b. Risk
c. Asset exposed to loss
d. Liability

15. Vandalism and Malicious Mischief (VMM) is an optional coverage that can be added by endorsement to which policy?

a. DP-1
b. DP-2
c. DP-3
d. DP-4

16. The DP-2 and DP-3 deny coverage for a dwelling vacant for more than 30 days. This restriction was amended in 2002 to how many consecutive days?

a. 45 days
b. 60 days
c. 75 days
d. 100 days

17. Which of the following exposures is excluded under collapse coverage?

a. Roofs
b. Storage sheds
c. Personal property in garages
d. Swimming pools

18. The purpose of insurance is to restore the insured's property back to what it was prior to the loss. This is defined by what term?

a. Insurance policy
b. Risk assumption
c. Risk management
d. Indemnity

19. An insurance policy contains multiple parts or sections to the document. The part that states the insurer will make payment or provide a service is known as what section?

a. Declarations
b. Conditions
c. Insuring agreement
d. Exclusions

20. Aaron is the warehouse manager for the midnight to 7 a.m. shift. One of his workers fell asleep while operating a piece of machinery during his shift and injured another worker. Even though Aaron was not the one who caused this accident, under what form of liability would he still potentially be held accountable?

a. Strict liability
b. Absolute liability
c. Vicarious liability
d. Definitive liability

21. Paul visited a wildlife safari to see the new lion exhibit. If Paul were to enter into the lion's gated area to help the safari worker with a feeding, he may not be able to sue the safari if anything wrong were to happen. Why would he lose the ability to sue?

a. Paul would have assumed strict or absolute liability due to the nature of the event.
b. Paul would have assumed vicarious liability due to the nature of the event.
c. The safari worker being there to help negates any right to sue.
d. The safari worker could sue Paul even though the entry was allowed.

22. Whose name always appears on the declarations page of an insurance policy?

a. Named insured
b. Legal representative for the named insured
c. Named insured's household members
d. There is no one named on the declarations page of an insurance policy.

23. A policy was written for a term of July 1, 2012, to July 1, 2013. An accident, which involved a completely covered loss, occurred on August 2, 2012. This accident, however, was not reported until April 1, 2014. The policy responded and paid this claim due to the fact that this was what type of policy?

a. Claims-made policy
b. Occurrence policy
c. Extended reporting policy
d. Claims-lapse policy

24. Which part or section of an insurance policy states both the insured and the insurer's rights and duties with respect to the insurance policy?

a. Policy exclusions
b. Policy conditions
c. Policy statement
d. Policy declarations

25. Patricia is a 50-year-old woman who teaches at a local college. She is a well-known and respected member of the community. When driving as the sun was setting, Patricia did not turn on her car lights. She caused an accident due to another operator not being able to see her car in the dark. Patricia is accused of acting in a careless and reckless manner. What is a term to define her actions?

a. Carelessness
b. Reckless action
c. Criminal activity
d. Negligence

26. What are documents which can be added to a policy either at inception or midterm that adds or amends the original policy?

a. Policy conditions
b. Policy exclusions
c. Policy definitions
d. Policy endorsements

27. Mary recently purchased her first home. She went to her local agent to obtain an insurance policy to ensure that if a loss occurred, she would be covered. Mary is said to have what in respect to this home?

    a. Insurable interest
    b. Insurable declaration
    c. Insurable responsibility
    d. Insurable commitment

28. Joseph was in a car accident in which his car was totaled. His insurance paid all of his repair bills, even though Joe was deemed not at fault. After Joe was indemnified by his insurance carrier, his carrier then started the process of being reimbursed for the claim from the at-fault party. This process of going after a third party for payment reimbursement is known as what process?

    a. Recovery
    b. Reimbursement assignment
    c. Subrogation
    d. Right to recovery

29. What type of policy will cover acceptable claims that are submitted to a carrier during the policy period and if the claim occurred during the stated time period on the policy?

    a. Occurrence policy
    b. Claims-made policy
    c. Claims-occurred policy
    d. Occurrence-made policy

30. A loss can arise for many different exposures or situations. What is a condition that leads to an increased possibility that a loss may occur?

    a. Hazard
    b. Risk
    c. Exposure
    d. Peril

31. Mrs. Smith was trying to demonstrate to her statistics class that if you toss a coin enough times, the results would be even on it landing heads or tails. What theory is Mrs. Smith teaching her students through this exercise?

    a. Normal distribution
    b. Standard deviation
    c. Law of large numbers
    d. Statistical probability

32. Gary owned a popular hardware store in the center of town. He had five employees working full time for the store. One night a fire broke out at a neighboring building and spread to Gary's store. The store was very badly damaged and would take months to restore before it could open again. Which of the following is a direct loss Gary felt from this fire?

    a. Damage to the building and inventory
    b. Loss in revenue
    c. Employees losing their income while the store is closed
    d. Extra expenses to house the inventory that was untouched until the building is repaired

33. Insurers use actual cash value (ACV) and replacement cost as two common methods to place value on exposures they are covering. ACV is the method insurers use when they are not willing to assume what hazard commonly associated with replacement cost?

    a. Physical hazard
    b. Morale hazard
    c. Moral hazard
    d. Legal hazard

34. Bill was interested in updating his house, as it was starting to look a little dated. He looked into all of his options and decided to refinance his mortgage, which would allow him to take money to put towards the repairs. To refinance, an appraiser came to Bill's house to see the state of the property, as well as to take notice of similar houses in the area to determine the worth of Bill's house. The appraiser came back to Bill with a number he calculated to accurately show what type of value of Bill's house?

    a. Stated value
    b. Actual cash value
    c. Replacement cost
    d. Market value

35. Megan purchased her first vehicle from the local car dealership. She called a local auto insurance agent and gave all the information regarding her driving history and details of her new auto. The agent was able to issue her a temporary agreement of coverage, valid until Megan was able to make it to the office to sign all necessary forms and pay the policy. What is the term for this temporary agreement of insurance coverage?

    a. Binder
    b. Endorsement
    c. Policy
    d. Notice of coverage form

36. What type of general liability coverage may be paid to cover specific expenses regardless of whether the insured is at fault or not?

    a. Auto repair
    b. Medical payments
    c. Loss of income
    d. Workers compensation

37. Mark and Jennifer are married and live in New York with their three children. Their oldest child, Kevin, was living eight months of the year in New Jersey at college. Mark's mother came into town and was staying with them for two weeks. During this two-week stay, Mark was shopping around for new insurance and the agent asked for a list of all insureds in the household. Taking in account Mark, Jennifer, his three kids (including Kevin), and Mark's mother, who is not considered an insured?

    a. Mark's mother
    b. Kevin
    c. All are insureds due to the nature of their relationship to Mark
    d. Kevin and Mark's mother

38. Kelsey was in a car accident in which her car was deemed a total loss. She called her insurance company to start the claims process and was told it would pay $3,500 for the loss. Kelsey was confused, as she had a policy where she assumed the insurer would pay for the full cost of the total loss of $7,700. Which type of policy did Kelsey most likely have?

    a. Agreed value
    b. Total value
    c. Stated value
    d. Collision value plus

39. Justin's house was destroyed by a fire. There were a few items that were damaged in the fire but Justin wanted to keep due to sentimental value. When the insurance claims adjuster came to visit the fire site, he took note of all the items Justin was keeping. The insurer will reduce the value of what the house is worth by the amount that the items Justin is keeping are worth. The value associated with these items is called what?

    a. Loss value
    b. Salvage value
    c. Keepsake value
    d. Recovery value

40. What is the term for the peril that directly causes the loss to occur? If there is more than one peril contributing to the loss, this is the term to define the peril most directly associated with the loss.

    a. Direct peril
    b. Loss cause
    c. Cause of concern
    d. Proximate cause

41. Insurance carriers require an insured to carry limits high enough to cover the cost to replace or repair the exposure if needed. What is the name given to this requirement by carriers?

    a. Value policy
    b. Limits equal/exposure limits
    c. Coinsurance plus
    d. Insurance to value/coinsurance

42. Bruce obtained an insurance policy for a property he planned to buy in the next two days. The effective date was to be the date the property was purchased. At settlement, the sellers backed away from the deal and Bruce was not able to purchase the property. He called his insurance agent and asked to cancel his policy. What type of cancellation will the insurer most likely process?

    a. Flat cancellation
    b. Short-rate cancellation
    c. Pro-rate cancellation
    d. It will not cancel due to the policy already being issued

43. ABC Insurance Inc. decided it no longer wanted to write policies for boats over 27 feet in length, effective immediately. ABC was going to cancel any policy in force that had this exposure as well. What type of cancellation would ABC process to return premium to these policyholders?

   a. Flat cancellation
   b. Short-rate cancellation
   c. Pro-rate cancellation
   d. It will not return premium to the policies holders

44. Sally had her auto policy for years through ABC Insurance. While talking with friends one day, Sally learned she could save money by switching her auto carrier to American Insurance. Sally signed a cancellation notice to ABC and was issued what type of cancellation policy?

   a. Flat cancellation
   b. Short-rate cancellation
   c. Pro-rate cancellation
   d. It will not cancel midterm just because an insured would like it to

45. Noelle was in a minor car accident in which she was deemed "at fault." After the car mechanic determined the extent of the damage, he submitted a $4,795 bill to Noelle's carrier. Noelle was then instructed to pay $500 and the carrier took care of the remaining portion of the bill. Noelle's $500 payment requirement is known as what?

   a. Accident pay
   b. Aggregate
   c. Deductible
   d. Premium due

46. The maximum amount of coverage an insurer will pay for a liability claim is defined as what term?

   a. Premium coverage
   b. Limits of coverage
   c. Limits of liability
   d. Policy value

47. Erin is a renewal underwriter. Part of her job is to re-underwrite risks each year to see if they still meet company and state guidelines. When reviewing one risk, Erin found out that a youthful operator received a DUI during the policy term. A DUI for a youthful operator is against company guidelines, and therefore Erin needed to get off of this risk. What type of notice would Erin send to fulfill state requirements as well as inform the insured that the insurer would not be renewing coverage?

   a. Cancellation
   b. Rescinding of coverages
   c. Policy void clause
   d. Nonrenewal

48. Martin was visiting a friend's house one night. During his stay, Martin was told that a neighbor had obtained a Super Bowl ring that was worth a lot of money. After Martin left his friend's house, he noticed the neighbor's house was dark and no one was home. Martin snuck in through a window and stole the Super Bowl ring. If caught, Martin will be convicted of what crime?

a. Burglary
b. Robbery
c. Theft
d. Malicious mischief

49. Mysterious disappearance is a broader form of coverage that is available by endorsement to a homeowners policy. This coverage is provided on an all-perils basis up to what limit?

a. $2,000
b. $2,500
c. $5,000
d. $5,500

50. Insurance policies contain a provision that requires the insured to notify the carrier that a claim has been made against the insured. This provision is known by what term?

a. Proof of claim
b. Documentation of claim
c. Claims discovery
d. Notice of claim

51. In order for an insurance carrier to begin the claims process, the insured must submit what formal statement?

a. Notice of claim
b. Proof of loss
c. Loss statement
d. No notice is needed to start the claims process

52. A standard mortgage clause gives the right to the mortgagee to recover after a loss, despite any neglect on the part of the insured. The mortgagee can only recover, however, if it is in possession of what?

a. The property
b. The insurance policy
c. The mortgage
d. The title of the land

53. Mary's house was badly damaged by a hurricane. A claims representative from her insurance company came out to inspect the damage and put a value on the loss. What Mary thought the value of her property was, and what the claims representative is stating the value to be, do not match. Mary is extremely upset over this dispute in value and wants another opinion. In accordance with Mary's rights under the insurance policy, she can request what option to get a second opinion on her loss value?

a. Appraisal
b. Outside source opinion
c. Value adjustment
d. Third-party adjuster

54. The policy that allows an insured to give or promise her insurance policy as collateral for a loan is known as what?

a. Promissory policy
b. Policy transfer
c. Assignment
d. Collateral policy

55. Lauren sent in an application for a homeowners policy. She answered each question accurately but failed to mention that her current policy was being non-renewed due to a bite claim from her three-year-old boxer terrier. If Lauren is issued the new policy but the carrier later finds out about her claim history, for what reason could it cancel Lauren's policy?

a. Misrepresentation
b. Concealment
c. Policy invalidation
d. Lying to licensed agent

56. Luke set up a meeting with an agent of ABC Insurance Inc. The purpose of this meeting was for Luke to obtain a personal umbrella policy to cover his personal assets and fulfill a requirement of his homeowners association. The agent went over various coverage forms and limits available to Luke, as well as premiums due. At the end of the meeting, Luke left with some paperwork to review and the agent was going to process a quote for Luke as well in the next day or so. If Luke agreed with the terms, he promised to pay his premium within the week. What one element of a contract is missing from Luke's situation?

a. Offer and acceptance
b. Two or more parties working towards an agreement
c. Consideration
d. Legal purpose

57. Abby sent in an application for a homeowners policy. She answered every question, but when asked if she had a previous claim history, she marked "no." Abby in fact was just non-renewed by her previous carrier for pipes bursting due to failure to maintain the heat. After the policy is issued, Abby's carrier learns of the past claim and cancels due to what reason?

a. Lying to a licensed agent
b. Concealment
c. Policy invalidation
d. Misrepresentation

58. Affirmative and promissory are two types of warranties. A warranty is the promise made by what party of the insurance contract?

    a. The insurer
    b. The agent representing the insurer
    c. The insured
    d. Both the insured and the agent

59. In 1970, this act was created to promote an accurate and fair process for collecting and using consumer credit reports. What is the formal name for this federal act?

    a. Fair Credit Reporting Act
    b. Federal Agency Reporting Act
    c. Federal Credit Care Act
    d. Fair Federal Care Act

60. Applications, inspections, credit reports, motor vehicle reports, etc., all make up different sources of what?

    a. Producer information
    b. Agent files
    c. Sources of underwriting information
    d. Client services

61. What law was passed in 1999 to lift many restrictions prohibiting insurance and financial companies from working with each other to act as a single entity? This act also prohibited the release of consumers' personal information to third parties unless the consumer opted out of this restriction.

    a. Fair Credit Reporting Act
    b. Gramm Leach Bliley Act
    c. Fair Federal Care Act
    d. Consumer Care Act

62. Many claims-made policies contain a provision that states that regardless of the claim being made during the policy period, the loss must not have occurred before a specific date stated on the policy. This provision is known as:

    a. Claims-occurred date
    b. Retroactive date
    c. Loss-occurred date
    d. Loss-reported date

63. An insurance company can offer a business what type of policy that would include both liability and property coverage?

    a. Commercial umbrella
    b. Business owner's umbrella
    c. Business package umbrella
    d. Commercial package policy

64. What type of policy is similar to a commercial package policy in that it combines both property and liability coverage in one policy, but is designed to meet the needs of eligible small businesses?

    a. Commercial umbrella
    b. Business owner's umbrella
    c. Business owner's policy
    d. Commercial package policy

65. For a small business to be eligible for a business owner's policy (BOP), the insurer looks not only at the size of the business but what other factor?

    a. The nature of the business
    b. The location of the business
    c. The amount of time the business has been in operation
    d. The average amount of people visiting the location per week

66. A business owner's policy (BOP) does not cover which of the following exposures?

    a. Personal injury
    b. Advertising injury protection
    c. Extra expenses
    d. Professional liability

67. All of the following are businesses that may be eligible for a business owner's policy (BOP) EXCEPT:

    a. Self-storage facilities
    b. Art galleries
    c. Cheese shops
    d. Drama schools

68. All of the following property coverages are automatically covered under the business owner's policy EXCEPT:

    a. Extra expenses
    b. Auto liability for business vehicles
    c. Valuable records
    d. Business income

69. What is a type of property insurance that provides coverage for certain covered items while they are in transit?

    a. Transportation insurance
    b. Moveable property insurance
    c. Inland marine coverage
    d. Transportation of personal property coverage

70. Besides covering property in transit, inland marine insurance can also cover what exposures?

    a. Means of communication
    b. Autos
    c. The home listed on the insurance
    d. Aircraft carrying the property in question

71. A floater policy is a type of inland marine policy that covers eligible personal property that is located where?

a. At the home listed on the application
b. Wherever the personal property may be (the only restriction being the policy territory)
c. Worldwide coverage exists
d. Only while in possession of the insured

72. What federally funded program was formed in response to a need by insureds for reasonably priced flood insurance?

a. Flood Nationwide Coverage
b. Specialty Flood Lines
c. National Flood Plan
d. National Flood Insurance Program

73. The National Flood Insurance Program provides coverage for direct damage to what types of property?

a. All of the insured's property while it is at the insured's location
b. The program provides direct and indirect damage coverage for the insured's personal property
c. The building and its contents
d. The program provides direct and indirect damage coverage for the insured's home building but not personal property

74. Logan was moving to Las Vegas, Nevada, for a job opportunity. Logan was concerned about the earthquakes he heard were a possibility in this area. When purchasing his homeowners policy, what should Logan ask for to make sure he has some coverage in the event of an earthquake?

a. An earthquake policy
b. Nothing, earthquake coverage is included
c. Nothing because earthquake coverage is not offered due to the frequency of earthquakes in Las Vegas
d. An endorsement to add earthquake coverage

75. Why do most insurance companies stop selling earthquake coverage for a period of time after an earthquake has occurred?

a. Because the insurance company is too busy handling claims to take on more risks
b. Because of the threat of aftershocks that come in the weeks following a sizeable earthquake
c. They are not allowed to by federal statute
d. Insurers do not stop selling earthquake insurance at all following an earthquake

76. Employee dishonesty coverage is an important coverage employers can obtain through a commercial crime policy. Employee dishonesty coverage provides coverage for theft of money, property, and what other exposure?

a. Securities
b. Other employees' personal property
c. Company card spending on personal needs
d. Company time unauthorized

77. Ben is the President of XYZ Logistics. He found out that one of his employees gained access to its payroll system and issued checks to himself and other co-workers. What type of insurance coverage does Ben need to have in place to protect himself or his company from this loss?

a. Payroll dishonesty coverage
b. Employee theft coverage
c. Forgery or alteration coverage
d. Employee forgery coverage

78. A surety bond is designed to protect which party of a contract?

a. The obligee
b. The principle
c. The surety
d. The surety bond protects all parties to a contract

79. A fidelity bond is designed to protect a business owner from what type of exposure?

a. Injured employees
b. Intentional acts of customers
c. Intentional acts of business partners
d. Dishonesty by employees

80. Kyle was injured while operating a piece of machinery in his company's warehouse. The injury left Kyle with permanent damage to his right shoulder, and the doctor told him he would never regain full range of motion for that arm. After two weeks of recovery at home, Kyle felt he was ready to return to work. Kyle's employer and his doctor worked to set up a meeting with a therapist to come to the warehouse and help Kyle learn how to perform his job with modifications for his injury. What type of rehabilitation process is Kyle's therapist helping him complete?

a. Machine rehabilitation
b. Vocational rehabilitation
c. Workers compensation rehabilitation
d. Modified job recovery

81. What type of professional insurance coverage protects the insured from liability resulting from an error or omission during the course of her professional job duty?

a. Employer's liability insurance
b. Employer's professional liability
c. Errors and omissions insurance
d. Employer's negligence insurance

82. The majority of medical malpractice insurance policies are written with what type of coverage trigger?

a. Occurrence trigger
b. Occurrence and claims-made triggers are equally common
c. There are no conditions regarding when the claim is made
d. Claims-made trigger

131

83. Intentional or criminal acts and sexual misconduct are two of the exclusions for medical malpractice exclusions. Provide one additional exclusion from the list below:
   a. Punitive damages
   b. Unintentional acts by a professional
   c. Patient chart error
   d. Insurance coverage discrepancies

84. What is one difference between director and officers (D&O) policies and commercial general liability policies (CGL)?
   a. D&O policies are written on an occurrence basis
   b. CGL policies are written on a claims-made basis
   c. D&O policies include defense cost inside the limits, not in addition to the policy limits
   d. CGL policies include defense cost inside the limits, not in addition to the policy limits

85. Director and officers liability insurance provides coverage for directors and officers of for-profit and not-for-profit organizations while these directors and officers are in what capacity?
   a. In the course of normal employment
   b. It is lifelong coverage for the directors and officers
   c. It does not cover not-for-profit organizations
   d. While the directors or officers are serving as an officer or on a board of directors

86. Medical malpractice insurance can be purchased through two sources. One source is a commercial insurer and the second source is known as what type of insurance company?
   a. Professional insurance association
   b. Bedpan mutual
   c. Medical professionals insurance
   d. Mutual insurance organizations

87. Sexual harassment, retaliation, discrimination, and wrongful termination are common types of claims employers may face during the employment process. What type of insurance is designed to cover against these types of claims?
   a. Workers' compensation
   b. Employment practices liability insurance
   c. Errors and omissions
   d. Employment errors liability insurance

88. Employment practices liability insurance (EPLI) provides defense costs for the insured in what capacity?
   a. Included in the limits
   b. Outside the limits
   c. Defense costs are not covered by an EPLI policy
   d. Defense costs can be purchased by endorsement to increase the limits

89. Employment practices liability insurance (EPLI) is written on the basis that the claim must be made during the policy period. This type of trigger is known as what type of policy?

    a. Occurrence basis
    b. Claims-required basis
    c. Claims-made basis
    d. EPLI is not made with the condition of when the claim must be made

90. Sarah was a victim of a car accident in which she severely injured her right leg. It took Sarah months of therapy to recover to nearly 100 percent. While in court to settle her claim, the judge offered Sarah $15,000 for her pain and suffering as a result of the accident. What type of damages was Sarah compensated for?

    a. General damages
    b. Punitive damages
    c. Special damages
    d. Pain and suffering damages

91. Cassie was a victim of an automobile accident in which substantial but not total damage was done to her car. Cassie sued the party at fault and was rewarded $7,525 to cover the cost of her vehicle and any other costs she incurred due to this accident. What type of damages was Cassie compensated for?

    a. General damages
    b. Punitive damages
    c. Total recovery damages
    d. Compensatory damages

92. Lindsey was driving home after a night out with friends. She had been drinking heavily and should not have been operating a vehicle. Lindsey caused a three-car accident in which there were injuries to each driver. While Lindsey was on trial for her actions, the other drivers were each rewarded $50,000 simply due to the fact that Lindsey broke the law and caused significant pain and suffering to the other drivers. This compensation awarded to the claimants is known as what form of damages?

    a. General damages
    b. Punitive damages
    c. Injured party damages
    d. Compensatory damages

93. Split limits is how an auto insurer represents which dollar amounts apply to each of the three limits stated on the policy. What is the best description of what the second limit of the split limits represents?

    a. The maximum amount that will be paid to the driver
    b. The maximum amount that will be paid to one injured person
    c. The maximum amount that will be paid to all injured people
    d. The maximum amount that will be paid for property that was damaged

94. Kerry was involved in an auto accident in which she was deemed at fault. The other driver Kerry hit had minor injuries but still required an ER visit and some additional testing. Which of the split limits would show the maximum amount insurance would pay to cover this one person who was injured?

   a. Limit 1
   b. Limit 2
   c. Limit 3
   d. Coverage is not available for a single injured operator in the split limits approach auto insurers use.

95. Samantha was found to be at fault for an accident resulting in total damage to both her vehicle and the vehicle she hit. While submitting her claim to the insurance company, Samantha asked her agent what was the total the company would pay for the damaged property. Which limit of the split limits on her policy will indicate the total amount Samantha's insurance company will pay for the property damage?

   a. Limit 1
   b. Limit 2
   c. Limit 3
   d. Coverage for property damage is excluded in a policy that has split limits

96. Tyler was walking down the stairs in his company's office building one day when he slipped and fell, fracturing his wrist. Tyler attempted to file a tort liability claim against his boss, but was told this type of lawsuit would not hold up in court. What is the reason Tyler is not allowed to make a tort liability claim against his employer?

   a. Employers are not responsible for their employees' actions.
   b. Tyler should have been more careful and is responsible for his own fall.
   c. Tyler is actually allowed to file this lawsuit and was inaccurately informed.
   d. Exclusive remedy bars workers from making tort liability claims against their bosses.

97. What are two reasons why the exclusive remedy provision may not hold up in barring employees from filing tort liability claims against their employers?

   a. There is nothing that could lift this provision.
   b. The employer failed to obtain insurance and there was willful negligence that led to the injury.
   c. The employer intentionally caused the injury and signed a waiver to allow the suit.
   d. The employee's injuries exceeded the amount of insurance available.

98. Benjamin was starting the process of building his house. His insurance agent suggested he obtain a policy that would provide property coverage while his house was being built. What type of insurance is Benjamin's agent suggesting he obtain?

   a. Course of construction insurance
   b. Construction coverage insurance
   c. Builder's coverage insurance
   d. Builder's risk insurance

99. Susie has an extensive collection of jewelry and fine arts. Susie's homeowners policy provides coverage for these exposures, but on a limited basis. What type of policy should Susie obtain to increase the coverage available for her jewelry and fine arts?

a. Personal articles floater
b. Personal property floater
c. Personal property extension endorsement
d. Specialized property coverage

100. An umbrella policy is a policy that can cover several different exposures on one policy. What is another name for this type of policy?

a. Blanket policy
b. All-exposures policy
c. Non-exclusive policy
d. Special forms policy

101. Barry was an experienced farmer but was behind on insuring all his exposures from potential damage. Barry lives in an area that is very susceptible to hailstorms and needed to make sure his crops were insured against the potential for hail damage. What type of policy should Barry look into getting?

a. Crop damage coverage
b. Hailstorm coverage
c. Crop-hail insurance
d. Hail damage insurance

102. Typically, the surviving spouse has how long to file for death benefits if her spouse died due to work-related injuries?

a. One month
b. Six months
c. There is no statute for applying for death benefits
d. One year

103. Personal injury is often combined with what other type of coverage in a standard commercial general liability (CGL) policy?

a. Medical payments
b. Auto payments
c. Advertising injury
d. Privacy coverage

104. Advertising injury coverage is designed to protect against all the following offenses EXCEPT:

a. Slander
b. Copyright infringement
c. Libel
d. Theft of goods

135

105. Insurance policies can vary in the way the deductible is handled or used. A policy in which the insured is required to reimburse the insurer for losses paid up to a stated amount is known as what type of deductible in an insurance policy?

a. Self-insured deductible
b. Annual aggregate deductible
c. Self-retention deductible
d. Annual self-retention deductible

106. Sean volunteered at a fundraiser over the weekend at his local community park. Sean was compensated for his time while at the fundraiser. When cleaning up from the event, Sean tripped over a vendor's tent and severely injured his wrist from the fall. Sean tried to pursue a workers' compensation claim from the park, but was denied. Why was Sean denied coverage?

a. A paid volunteer is excluded under workers' compensation laws.
b. The event was over and therefore coverage was void.
c. Sean was responsible for his own actions based on his role as a volunteer.
d. Sean would not have been denied workers' compensation benefits.

107. Hillary was driving her new car on a country road when a deer ran out in front of her. Hillary hit the deer and sustained damage to her auto. What type of coverage would apply to this type of accident?

a. Collision coverage
b. Animal collision coverage
c. Animal damage
d. Other-than-collision coverage

108. Brenton's vehicle was damaged due to an accident in which he was at fault and it would take about two weeks to be fully repaired. Brenton asked his agent if he would be reimbursed for the cost of renting an auto during the two-week period. Would his agent say yes if he had an unendorsed auto policy?

a. Yes. Rental reimbursement is automatically included in any auto policy.
b. Yes. Rental reimbursement is included due to the length of time Brenton needs to rent a vehicle exceeding the one-week minimum.
c. No. Rental reimbursement coverage is only provided if it was added by endorsement to an auto policy.
d. No. Rental reimbursement is never an option if you are deemed at fault for the accident.

109. Garagekeepers coverage is designed to protect what group of insureds from liability exposures?

a. Parking garage owners
b. Automobile dealers with a service department
c. A person housing a friend's auto while he is on vacation
d. Car wash services

110. Joseph is a farmer who is seeking crop-hail insurance to protect his exposure to the high frequency of hail in his area. When Joseph meets with his agent, he asks how the rate for crop-hail insurance is determined. Joseph's agent states that the rate is triggered by what reasoning?

a. Past losses of the insured
b. Past losses in the county or township
c. Whatever the insurance carrier deems appropriate
d. The federal government sets the rate

111. All of the following are covered as "hired auto" on an automobile policy EXCEPT:

a. Car borrowed from a household member
b. Car borrowed by insured from leasing center
c. Car rented from leasing center for family vacation
d. Car hired by insured from leasing center for personal use

112. Sam purchased a mobile home as a house his family could use while visiting his in-laws a state away. Does Sam have to obtain a specialized policy for this type of home?

a. Yes, coverage is only available for mobile homes on specialized forms.
b. No, coverage can be on a specialized form policy or as an endorsement to a standard homeowners policy.
c. Yes, coverage is not available on a homeowners policy due to the foundation requirement.
d. No, coverage for this type of exposure is not available.

113. David purchased a new vehicle for his 16-year-old son. David currently insures two other autos with ABC Insurance. Does coverage apply for the new vehicle as soon as David acquires the auto from the dealership?

a. Coverage applies only if David's policy includes a new car endorsement.
b. Coverage applies, but prompt notification of the carrier is required.
c. Coverage does not apply unless the carrier is notified before the purchase.
d. Coverage does not apply since David's son will require his own policy.

114. Rebecca was driving to work when she was hit at a red light. The driver who hit her did not carry insurance. She submitted a claim to her own insurance carrier and was covered for this accident. What type of coverage did Rebecca have on her auto policy that allowed her to collect from her own carrier even though she was not at fault for the accident?

a. No-fault insurance
b. All carriers provide coverage automatically against uninsured operators
c. Uninsured motorist coverage
d. Rebecca's carrier and all carriers would exclude coverage due to her being not at fault for the accident

115. A DP-2 insurance policy is written to provide coverage desired by most landlords. A DP-2 specifically lists all the perils that the policy will insure against. What is another name for this type of policy that lists all covered perils?

a. Open perils
b. Listed perils
c. Specified perils
d. Named perils

116. Manufacturers need coverage to protect themselves against claims arising from their business. What policy is written to specifically protect against claims due to products manufactured and sold?

a. Products sold liability
b. Products and completed operations liability
c. Product completion liability
d. Manufacturers coverage

117. Patrick is the CEO of a major marketing firm in the city. As part of his compensation package, he is given a fully paid company car for his own use. Patrick, while he does have other cars in his household, still needs to carry adequate insurance coverage as a driver of the company vehicle. What type of endorsement should he obtain to cover his needs as an operator of the company vehicle?

a. Drive other car endorsement
b. Business car coverage endorsement
c. He does not need an endorsement to cover this need, as his auto policy will automatically cover it
d. Business risk coverage endorsement

118. Mary was down on her luck and in desperate need of money to pay her bills. Mary was so desperate that she went into a bank with a gun to demand money. Mary when caught was convicted of what crime?

a. Theft
b. Burglary
c. Robbery
d. Firearm abuse

119. What is a key coverage provided by a commercial crime policy?

a. Employee dishonesty coverage
b. Employee false accusations
c. Employee wrongful termination
d. Employee dishonesty and theft coverage

120. Once a loss occurs, it is not just the insurer that has a duty to act, but the insured as well. All of the following are duties of the insured after a loss EXCEPT:

a. Protect the property from further damage
b. Complete all repairs and wait for reimbursement from insurer
c. Complete temporary repairs if needed to protect the property
d. Keep a record of all receipts from anything purchased to complete repairs

Answer Key and Explanations

1. B: HO-4 and HO-6 are not designed to be exclusive for owner-occupied dwellings. HO-4 was formed to cover a tenant's personal property. An HO-6 provides personal property coverage for an owner-occupied condominium, and also can provide coverage for co-owners of this condominium who reside there.

2. C: The HO-8 policy form. This policy form is designed to provide dwelling, personal property, and other structures coverage for an owner-occupied dwelling. The dwellings eligible for an HO-8 do not meet the standards that insurers require for the other five policy forms.

3. A: HO-4. An HO-4 is designed to cover a tenant's personal property, but does not cover the dwelling itself. This coverage is provided on a named-perils basis.

4. A: HO-5 provides dwelling, other structures, and coverage on an open-perils basis. The HO-5 provides the broadest coverage form of all the HO policy forms.

5. B: Glass breakage is a peril that is covered on a broad-perils-form basis. Additional perils covered on broad form include ice and snow weight, freezing of pipes, collapse, falling objects, and electrical damage.

6. D: Theft is not covered on an unendorsed DP-3. Garages and storage sheds fit under the "other structures" definition if they are on the insured's premises. Debris removal is paid in the limit assigned to the property that sustained the loss.

7. A: Coverage A – Land is not a coverage under a DP-3. The dwelling form includes five coverages: Coverage A – Dwelling, Coverage B – Other Structures, Coverage C – Personal Property, Coverage D – Fair Rental Value, and Coverage E – Additional Living Expense.

8. B: Special forms coverage is coverage on a DP policy form that combines broad-form perils and open perils. The open perils are for the dwelling and other structures while the broad form is provided for personal property.

9. B: Coverage C – Personal Property covers personal property while at the location listed on the DP-3 policy. This does not provide full coverage or coverage at all for personal property while away from the location on the policy.

10. C: Pure risk. Pure risk is always undesirable to an investor. A pure risk results in either a loss or no loss. A speculative risk has the chance there will be a gain.

11. A: Moral hazard. A moral hazard is defined as intentionally causing, fabricating, or exaggerating a loss. An example of a moral hazard is someone exaggerating the extent of damage from an accident in order to receive more money from the at-fault parties' insurance carrier.

12. D: Physical hazard. An insured who fails to maintain his property can create a physical hazard. Physical hazards can increase the frequency of losses and lead to an increase in claims.

13. B: Morale hazard. Sara acted carelessly because she knew her insurance would cover any losses from a robbery to her store. Sara is acting in a reckless manner that may lead to insurance claims being paid that could have been otherwise avoided.

139

14. A: Peril. A peril is defined as the cause of loss. A peril, along with the asset exposed to loss and the financial consequence of the loss, all make the elements of a loss exposure.

15. A: DP -1. DP-1 policies are able to add VMM coverage by endorsement. VMM is automatically included in the other dwelling policy forms.

16. B: 60 days. In 2002, the definition of "vacancy" was amended to 60 days. This has helped make this form less restrictive and open it up to more insureds for coverage.

17. D: Swimming pools. Swimming pools are excluded from coverage when a loss is experienced due to collapse. It is important as an insurance professional that you accurately explain what is excluded from specific coverages when a potential insured is letting you know all of her personal exposures.

18. D: Indemnity is the main purpose of obtaining an insurance policy. Indemnity is the term that seeks to restore the insured back to the state his property was in prior to the loss.

19. C: Insuring agreement. The insuring agreement is part of the insurance policy that states that the insurer will make a payment or provide the insured with services (subject to any conditions or exclusion).

20. C: Vicarious liability. Aaron as the manager, or one in charge of the employees, can be held liable for the actions of his workers. A court could argue that Aaron should have known his worker was tired and unable to run the equipment in a safe manner.

21. A: Strict or absolute liability. Paul working with the lions assumes strict or absolute liability. Lions are extremely dangerous animals that you can have little to no control over. Paul entering this situation on his own terms knew the inherent danger.

22. A: Named insured. The named insured is always found on the declarations page of the insurance policy. This placement is to name who is the owner of the policy, who is to pay the premium, and who is to collect any premium paid back due to cancellations.

23. B: Occurrence policy. The policy responded to this claim due to the accident occurring during the policy period, which is defined as an "occurrence policy." Had the accident occurred outside the policy term, it would have been denied. An occurrence policy differs from a claims-made policy because in an occurrence policy, the claim can be submitted after the policy expires.

24. B: Policy conditions. The policy conditions section of an insurance policy will state the rights and duties assigned to both the insured and the insurer with respect to the policy in question. Both rights and duties of each party are dependent on the other party fulfilling his duties, and if one party neglects his responsibilities, it may relieve the other party of his duties.

25. D: Negligence. Negligence can be defined as failure to act in a reasonable manner. Patricia knew well enough that her lights should have been turned on in those driving conditions. If she had acted with the reasonable degree of care owed as a driver, she could have probably avoided causing the accident.

26. D: Policy endorsements. An endorsement can be attached to a policy at inception or added midterm. An endorsement modifies the policy in some way, either by adding or deleting a coverage or exposure. An example would be that if an insured purchased another location mid-policy period, she could submit to the insurer to have this location added to the current policy.

27. A: Insurable interest. Mary has an insurable interest in her newly purchased home. If there were to be a loss to this location, Mary herself would suffer a direct financial loss.

28. C: Subrogation. Subrogation is the right of the insurer to go after the at-fault party's insurer for payment reimbursement. Joseph's insurer paid his repair cost even though he was not at fault for the accident. The insurer, however, does not need to be out this claims money and is legally able to recover its expenses from the at-fault party's insurer.

29. B: Claims-made policy. A claims-made form is a type of liability coverage policy that covers a claim made during the policy period. This claim must be submitted to the carrier during the policy period and the claim must have occurred on or after the retroactive date of the policy. This differs from an occurrence policy, in which the claim can be made after the policy period ends.

30. A: Hazard. A hazard is a condition that can lead to the increased chance that a loss will occur. Hazards can be classified in three ways: moral, physical, and morale. An insured should do her best to avoid any hazard, if possible, to reduce the likelihood of a loss.

31. C: Law of large numbers. The law of large numbers is used in insurance the same way Mrs. Smith is using her coin example. Insurers use this theory to determine how likely it is that a claim will occur. They can use data such as "one in 50 houses will experience a fire." The insurer will then write 50 insurance policies to ensure that the 50 premiums collected can cover the one fire.

32. A: Damage to the building and inventory. The fire caused a direct loss of physical damage to the store building itself and the damaged inventory. There is a reduction in value to the store and the inventory, if not completely damaged by the loss. Loss in revenue, employees losing their pay, and the extra expenses are all results of the loss, but they are indirect losses.

33. C: Moral hazard. When an exposure is covered on a replacement-cost basis, the exposure is repaired or replaced with similar quality materials. An insured could potentially notice his car has some wear and tear over the years and a moral hazard could arise because he wants his car to be replaced with a new one. With actual cost value (ACV), the insured only recovers the replacement cost minus depreciation. The insured with ACV in the same scenario with the car would mostly likely not receive as much claims compensation.

34. D: Market value. The market value is the price Bill, or another buyer, would have to pay to purchase the home today. Bill's appraiser took the value he saw in Bill's house and compared it to similar homes in the area to determine the market value of Bill's house. Market value is important to refinancing as well as selling or buying a home. The market value can go up or down depending not only on the house itself, but also the area where the home is located.

35. A: Binder. A binder is a temporary form of insurance coverage agreement. Megan still needs to fulfill all the insurer's requirements of forms and pay before the coverage can be fully issued and out of binder status. The coverage becomes firm once the binder is issued into a full policy.

36. B: Medical payments. Medical payments are a type of general liability coverage that will pay the immediate medical bills needed if a person is hurt on the insured's premises. The insured does not need to be found liable for this coverage to apply. An example would be if a child was playing in the insured's yard and fell and required stitches. The medical payments of the insured would cover the child's emergency room visit.

37. A: Mark's mother. An insured is defined as any member of the household. Kevin, while living most of the time at college, is still considered a household member due to the nature of him being a student and his parents' address still being his "primary location." Mark's mother, while she may be covered if she operated his vehicle as a permissive user insured, is not considered an insured of the household. A two-week visit does not change the fact that she lives and uses another address as her main residence.

38. C: Stated value. Kelsey had a stated value policy from her insurance carrier. This type of policy states the maximum amount it will pay out for a claim, but it does not guarantee to pay up to that amount. A stated value policy will often pay less because the insurer can pay the lesser amount of the replacement cost of the car or its actual cash value.

39. B: Salvage value. Salvage value is defined as the scrap value of damaged goods or damaged property. Because Justin is keeping this damaged property, the insured will not be required to count these items in the total loss of the house.

40. D: Proximate cause. Proximate cause is the peril that directly causes the loss to occur.

41. D: Insurance to value/coinsurance. Insurance carriers require limits high enough to cover the cost to replace or repair the exposure if needed. Some insurance policies require limits equal to 100 percent of the cost of the exposure, while other policies may just require 80 percent. It is important to understand this requirement when determining the limit needs of each insured.

42. A: Flat cancellation. The insurer will be able to flat cancel Bruce's policy because he never maintained ownership of this property and therefore the policy was never needed. A flat cancellation returns full premium as if the policy was never issued.

43. C: Pro-rate cancellation. The insurer will have to issue a pro-rate cancellation, as it is the party terminating coverage, not the insured. The insured will be reimbursed the full premium for the unexpired length of the policy term.

44. B: Short-rate cancellation. Sally will be issued the amount of premium for the unexpired portion of her policy minus a penalty for cancelling the policy. There is a penalty associated with the cancellation because Sally is the party cancelling, not the insurance company.

45. C: Deductible. A deductible is the amount noted on the policy that the insured agrees to pay to cover part of the loss. Noelle's $500 deductible payment will be subtracted from the total bill due to pay her for her car repairs. As part of the insurance contract, Noelle's carrier will pay the remaining portion of the bill.

46. C: Limits of liability. The limits of liability an insured purchases for his liability policy is the maximum amount an insurer will pay for a covered claim. The limits of liability for some cases include defense costs, but for some policies, defense costs may be paid in addition to the limits of liability.

47. D: Nonrenewal. A nonrenewal notice is a formal statement that coverage will not be renewed for another policy term. Nonrenewals must be sent to fulfill state requirements of notice to the insured, but must also be sent within the time frame the state requires.

48. A: Burglary. Martin would be found guilty of burglary because he entered a person's property without permission and stole from this property. If Martin is not caught in this illegal act, the property owner's insurance carrier may have to pay for this loss.

49. B: $2,500. Mysterious disappearance can be a coverage added by endorsement to a homeowners policy. This coverage could be needed for insureds whose business is selling goods out of their homes.

50. D: Notice of claim. The notice of claim provision is an essential part of an insurance policy. This provision puts the responsibility on the insured to make the insurance carrier aware of the pending claim.

51. B: Proof of loss. An insured is obligated as part of the insurance policy to provide the insurance company with a proof of loss. An insurance company cannot begin to investigate the claim for coverage or denial until the proof of loss statement is received.

52. C: The mortgage. The mortgagee is entitled to recover from the loss if the policy is considered void due to an act by the insured. The mortgagee is bound by the same conditions and exclusions of an insurance policy, but is seen as a separate interest in the property.

53. A: Appraisal. An appraisal is a right given by the insurance policy to ask for a third party's opinion on the value of the loss. This right is practiced when the insured does not agree with the value the insurer is putting on the loss sustained. The insurer cannot deny an appraisal, as it is a right stated in the insurance contract.

54. C: Assignment. Assignment is the right given by some insurance policies to give or promise your own policy as a form of collateral to obtain a loan. Assignment is not allowed in all types of policies, but is common in life insurance policies. A lender may require an assignment agreement if the insured's business is dependent on the insured's presence and therefore his death would mean the business could not survive. The end of the business would not allow the loan to be paid back to the insurer, which is where the assignment of the insurance policy would be used to pay the loan.

55. B: Concealment. While Lauren did answer every question on the homeowners application accurately, she failed to mention a claim that is relevant to this type of policy. Any facts that could be used to determine eligibility of a risk must be disclosed at the time of quoting or the insurer may have the right to cancel.

56. A: Offer and acceptance. Elements of an insurance contract include two or more parties in agreement, legal purpose, offer and acceptance, and consideration. Luke's legal purpose in obtaining his umbrella policy was to fulfill a requirement of his homeowners association. The agent and Luke are the two parties who are working towards an agreement and contract of insurance coverage. The element of consideration is the exchange of money for the premium from Luke for the coverage the insurance company is going to provide. The fourth element of a contract – offer and acceptance – is not yet met because Luke has not yet agreed to final terms to issue the policy or contract.

57. D: Misrepresentation. Abby did not answer each question on her insurance application truthfully. When an insurer learns the insured has misrepresented her risk, the insurer has the right to cancel. The insurer has the right to cancel because had it known about the previous claim; it may have never written Abby's policy.

58. C: The insured. The insured is promising, or making a warranty, that all facts presented to the insurer are accurate and honest. The insurer is relying on this warranty when it makes the decision to underwrite this risk. A warranty is generally required on information that could be a deciding factor to accept the risk – as in a past claims history or not listing members of the household with poor driving records.

59. A: Fair Credit Reporting Act. The Fair Credit Reporting Act is a federal act that was enacted in 1970. This act defines the legal procedures and standards for using consumer reports, specifically credit reports. The report allows customer to opt out of the sharing of her information between affiliates of the organization pulling the credit information.

60. C: Sources of underwriting information. Applications, inspections, credit reports, and motor vehicle reports all make up informational sources that can help underwrite a risk. An underwriter sometimes needs multiple sources of information in order to make an informed decision to write an account. An example would be the personal umbrella product. To write a personal umbrella, insurers will need to review the application for all exposures noted as well as motor vehicle reports to review the insured's driving history. The underwriter may also order an inspection of the location to be covered.

61. B: Gramm Leach Bliley Act. The Gramm Leach Bliley Act was enacted in 1999 to set forth a standard for how different agencies and institutions interact with each other. The act also forced financial and banking companies to be upfront with consumers about sharing their information with third parties. It prohibited the release of consumers' personal information to third parties unless the consumer opted out of this restriction. This act is also known as the Financial Services Modernization Act of 1999.

62. B: Retroactive date. The retroactive date is a policy provision on claims-made policies that restricts coverage to claims that are made during the policy period, and the loss must have occurred after a specified date named on the policy. The purpose of the provision is to exclude losses the insured knows about and is buying a policy in anticipation of a claim being reported in the near future.

63. D: Commercial package policy. A commercial package policy is a means for business owners to package two or more coverage parts into one policy. This can include property, liability, inland marine, farm, crime, etc. Often a package policy is desirable to an insured because it may have a lower premium due than if multiple separate policies are written.

64. C: Business owner's policy. A business owner's policy (BOP) is a package policy that offers more specialized and unique features for a small business. Like the commercial package policy, the BOP can often offer a less expensive policy as compared to writing multiple monoline policies to fit all the needs of the insured.

65. A: The nature of the business. For a small business to be eligible for a BOP, the business must not exceed $3 million in gross sales annually and the property location itself cannot be larger than 25,000 square feet. The BOP is intended to cover small businesses with commercial locations, and is not necessarily intended for home-based businesses.

66. D: Professional liability. The BOP is not intended to provide any professional liability for the business owner (the insured). The liability portion of the BOP does provide coverage for personal injury and advertising injury protection. The property portion will provide coverage automatically for extra expenses on the BOP.

67. A: Self-storage facilities. A self-storage facility is ineligible for a BOP regardless of its size and gross annual income. The art gallery, cheese store, and drama school may all be eligible for a BOP depending on their size and the overall nature of the business.

68. B: Auto liability for business vehicles. Extra expenses, valuable records, and business income are all automatically included under the business owner's policy. This differs from the home business policy, which covers these exposures only through optional endorsements.

69. C: Inland marine coverage. Inland marine coverage is available to cover certain types of property while they are being transported. Inland marine forms usually provide broader coverage than property forms.

70. A: Means of communication. Inland marine insurance is designed to cover not only transported property, but also means of communication. These communication methods can include radio towers and televisions.

71. B: Wherever the personal property may be. This, however, is restricted to the territory the policy covers; as is, the policy may say "all U.S. states and territories." The floater policy may be specialized in many ways, including an equipment floater, installation floater, etc.

72. D: National Flood Insurance Program. The National Flood Insurance Program (NFIP) was enacted in 1968 in response to a need by insureds for reasonably priced flood insurance. This program is federally funded and available for specific areas that participate in this government-sponsored program.

73. C: The building and its contents. The National Flood Insurance Program provides coverage for direct damage to the insured's building and its contents. There is no coverage provided for any losses suffered as an indirect loss stemming from the flood.

74. D: An endorsement to add earthquake coverage. Earthquake coverage is excluded on most property policies, and the only way to secure the coverage is through an endorsement. The endorsement can be quite expensive in areas where the threat of an earthquake is high.

75. B: Because of the threat of aftershocks that come in the weeks following a sizeable earthquake. While the initial earthquake may cause severe damage, the aftershocks that can follow may cause even more widespread devastation. Insurers stop selling insurance right after the initial earthquake because they are trying to avoid those who are buying insurance or increasing limits because they know there is a high chance of an aftershock.

76. A: Securities. Employee dishonesty coverage is an important coverage for employers to obtain. Employee crime can happen in any environment. While it is of utmost importance to try to prevent theft, insurance must be in place to cover extreme cases. Theft of money, property, and securities are coverages provided by the employee dishonesty coverage policy.

77. C: Forgery or alteration coverage. Forgery or alteration coverage protects the insured from checks, including payroll, being processed with a forged signature. This coverage also protects against checks made payable to a fake entity or any alteration to the amount of the check.

78. A: The obligee. A surety bond is designed to protect the obligee in the event that the principal cannot or does not perform their part of the contract. The surety is the party that will uphold the contractual agreement on the part of the principal.

79. D: Dishonesty by employees. A fidelity bond protects employers from money, securities, and property losses that are the result of employee dishonesty. Fidelity bonds are just one type of insurance policy designed to protect the company against crime-related activity in the workplace.

145

80. B: Vocational rehabilitation. Vocational rehabilitation is the process of helping injured workers return to their jobs with some modifications to how they perform their job responsibilities. This process is often completed with the help of a therapist under the regulation of the state's Workers Compensation Act.

81. C: Errors and omissions insurance (E&O). Errors and omissions insurance protects against financial losses due to an error or omission by the insured while acting in a professional capacity. This coverage does not apply for property damage or bodily injury.

82. D: Claims-made trigger. Sometimes coverage is available for medical malpractice insurance on an occurrence basis, but most policies are written on a claims-made basis. This coverage is intended for physicians and surgeons to protect from E&O claims.

83. A: Punitive damages. Punitive damages, sexual misconduct, and intentional or criminal acts are excluded from the medical malpractice insurance policy. Unintentional acts are not excluded because intent is not a necessary element of malpractice. Patient chart error is not excluded because charts are typically not monitored by the physician or surgeon but rather by office staff or nurses. Finally, insurance coverage discrepancies have to do with the insurance company in question, not the insured (physician or surgeon).

84. C: D&O Policies include defense cost inside the limits, not in addition to the policy limits. This is a major difference between the two because defense cost can be substantial and therefore decrease the limits left to cover the claim drastically. This is a disadvantage to the insured over a CGL policy.

85. D: While the directors or officers are serving as an officer or on a board of directors. The directors and officers must be serving on a board or as an officer for coverage to apply under a director and officers liability insurance policy. This coverage can apply for both for-profit and not-for-profit organizations.

86. B: Bedpan mutual. Bedpan mutual is the name for a physician-owned insurance company. This type of insurer is available in most states to offer medical malpractice insurance for physicians and surgeons needing coverage for E&O exposures.

87. B: Employment practices liability insurance. Employment practices liability insurance (EPLI) is designed to protect employers against claims arising from wrongful acts in the course of the employment process. EPLI can also provide protection against inappropriate acts at work such as invasion of privacy.

88. A: Included in the limits. Employment practices liability policies are written with defense costs within the limits, also known as "shrinking limits." Defense costs can be quite large and therefore may significantly reduce the amount of limits available to cover a claim.

89. C: Claims-made basis. Employment practices liability policies are written on a claims-made basis. A claims-made basis requires the claim to have been made during the stated policy period. The claim must have occurred on or after the retroactive date and before the policy period ends.

90. A: General damages. General damages are awarded to an injured party to compensate for the pain and suffering experienced as a result of an accident or injury. General damages are given as a monetary reward.

91. D: Compensatory damages. Cassie was rewarded the total amount it would take to account for the actual loss sustained. Compensatory damages can include both general and special damages.

92. B: Punitive damages. The judge, by awarding $50,000 to each claimant, intended to punish Lindsey for her wrongful acts. Punitive damages are also known as "exemplary damages" and are excluded by most umbrella policies.

93. C: The maximum amount that will be paid to all injured people. Three separate limits apply when the auto insurer is offering split limits on an insurance policy. The second limit represents the maximum dollar amount the insurer is willing to pay to cover all people who were injured in the automobile accident.

94. A: Limit 1. Limit 1, of the three split limits offered in auto insurance, is designed to represent the maximum dollar amount the insurer will pay to any one person injured as a result of an automobile accident. Limit 2 represents the total amount to be paid to all injured persons.

95. C: Limit 3. Limit 3 indicates the total amount that the insurance company will pay for property damage claims. This limit applies does not just apply to vehicles damaged, but to any property that may be damaged as a result of the accident.

96. D: Exclusive remedy bars workers from making tort liability claims against their bosses. Exclusive remedy excludes such employees from making tort liability claims because the benefits provided under the workers compensation policy are the only benefits typically provided to an injured employee. This provision is found in every state.

97. B: The employer failed to obtain insurance and there was willful negligence that led to the injury. Two of the reasons that allow the bar preventing employees from filing a tort liability claim to be lifted is if the employer failed to obtain the proper workers compensation insurance and was deemed willfully negligent. Another reason this provision could be lifted is the dual-capacity doctrine, which allows the employee to file suit against the employer in a third-party capacity.

98. D: Builder's risk insurance. Builder's risk insurance is designed to protect against damage that may occur during the course of construction. This policy protects the insured's insurable interest in the building, fixtures, and equipment being used to complete the construction.

99. A: Personal articles floater. Susie should obtain a personal articles floater to secure the insurance limits needed to properly cover her jewelry and fine arts. A personal articles floater can be added by endorsement to a homeowners policy and is provided on an all-risks basis.

100. A: Blanket policy. A blanket policy is similar to an umbrella policy in that it is one insurance policy written to cover multiple different exposures. The different exposures covered may include locations, properties, goods being transported, etc.

101. C: Crop-hail insurance. Barry needs to obtain crop-hail insurance to protect his exposure to the high frequency of hailstorms in his region. This type of insurance can be purchased from private insurers that handle the marketing and underwriting for this exposure.

102. D: One year. A spouse typically has one year to file for death benefits from a work-related death. The statute is set to process claims as soon as possible after a death and to also try to prevent fraudulent claims from being submitted years after a death occurred.

103. C: Advertising injury. Advertising injury and personal injury are often combined on a standard CGL policy. Advertising injury provides coverage for the insured's use of advertising for his services or goods sold.

104. D: Theft of goods. Advertising injury is designed to protect the insured from claims of slander, libel, copyright infringement, privacy invasion, etc. This coverage is found on a standard commercial general liability (CGL) policy.

105. B: Annual aggregate deductible. A policy with an annual aggregate deductible requires the insured to reimburse the insurer for paid losses up to a stated amount. After this amount is reached, the insurer is responsible for any more losses that may occur in the policy period.

106. A: A paid volunteer is excluded under workers compensation laws. An employee by definition under workers compensation laws includes day labor, borrow employees, part-time employees, unpaid volunteer employees, etc., but workers compensation does not provide coverage when volunteers are paid for their work. The park's insurance will probably pay for Sean's immediate medical care, but further coverage would be excluded under the workers compensation definition of who is an insured.

107. D: Other-than-collision coverage. Hillary's auto policy would need to have other-than-collision coverage in order for her accident to have coverage. Other-than-collision coverage is provided on an "all risks" basis for perils other than collision. Some of the perils include contact with animals, glass breakage, and water and flood damage.

108. C: No. Rental reimbursement coverage is only provided if it was added by endorsement to an auto policy. Brenton would not have coverage for his rental car because he did not purchase the optional endorsement to his auto policy. Rental reimbursement is an important endorsement to insurers because accidents involving rental vehicles can be quite costly if the vehicle requires extensive repairs and there is no deductible applied with this coverage.

109. B: Automobile dealers with a service department. Automobile dealers who also run a service department or body repair shop should obtain garagekeepers coverage to protect from liability exposures that could arise while the auto is in the care of the dealer. Liability on the part of the insured has to be proven in order for coverage to apply.

110. B: Past losses in the county or township. Crop-hail insurance rates are triggered by the loss exposure the township or county has experienced in the past. The federal government does not subsidize this type of insurance.

111. A: Car borrowed from a household member. A car that the insured borrows, leases, or rents from a household member does not fit the definition of a "hired auto." Other autos that are not considered "hired autos" are ones the insured borrows, leases, or rents from partners or employees.

112. B: No, coverage can be on a specialized form policy or as an endorsement to a standard homeowners policy. Sam does not need to search for a specialized policy to cover his mobile home if his agent can write a homeowners policy with an endorsement for mobile homes. A mobile home does require unique coverage needs that are not provided for by an unendorsed homeowners policy.

113. B: Coverage applies, but prompt notification of the carrier is required. Insurance carriers often do not require notification prior to the purchase of an additional vehicle, but most require notification within a specified time period. It is important to note when purchasing a new auto what your specific carrier requires in terms of notification process in order to maintain property coverage.

114. C: Uninsured motorist coverage. Rebecca had purchased uninsured motorist coverage when she obtained her auto insurance policy. This coverage steps in when at-fault operators have failed to obtain auto insurance coverage of their own. Uninsured motorist coverage is sometimes automatically included in a policy, but often needs to be purchased as an added coverage.

115. D: Named perils. DP-2 and DP-1 policies are both written on a named-perils basis. Named perils specify in a list exactly which perils the policy will insure against. If a peril is not listed on the policy, the policy will not provide coverage for it.

116. B: Products and completed operations liability. Products and completed operations liability is purchased by wholesalers, distributors, and manufacturers to protect themselves against claims arising due to injuries caused by their products. This type of coverage only applies after the products are complete.

117. A: Drive other car endorsement. A drive other car endorsement is an endorsement to extend coverage to a non-owned auto driven by either the insured or their spouse for personal use. Coverage does not apply while the insured is in the business of servicing or repairing autos.

118. C: Robbery. Mary would be convicted of robbery because of threatening force by having a gun. This force was used with the intent of committing theft of money.

119. A: Employee dishonesty coverage. Employee dishonesty coverage is an important coverage that employers can obtain in their commercial crime policies. This coverage provides against theft of securities, property, or money.

120. B: Complete all repairs and wait for reimbursement from insurer. The insured is not typically supposed to completely repair the damaged property and then wait for reimbursement from the insurer. The insured is, however, supposed to protect the damaged property from sustaining any further damage. Sometimes to protect the property, temporary repairs may be necessary. The insured should keep any receipts from making these temporary repairs to possibly be reimbursed by the insurer.

How to Overcome Test Anxiety

Just the thought of taking a test is enough to make most people a little nervous. A test is an important event that can have a long-term impact on your future, so it's important to take it seriously and it's natural to feel anxious about performing well. But just because anxiety is normal, that doesn't mean that it's helpful in test taking, or that you should simply accept it as part of your life. Anxiety can have a variety of effects. These effects can be mild, like making you feel slightly nervous, or severe, like blocking your ability to focus or remember even a simple detail.

If you experience test anxiety—whether severe or mild—it's important to know how to beat it. To discover this, first you need to understand what causes test anxiety.

Causes of Test Anxiety

While we often think of anxiety as an uncontrollable emotional state, it can actually be caused by simple, practical things. One of the most common causes of test anxiety is that a person does not feel adequately prepared for their test. This feeling can be the result of many different issues such as poor study habits or lack of organization, but the most common culprit is time management. Starting to study too late, failing to organize your study time to cover all of the material, or being distracted while you study will mean that you're not well prepared for the test. This may lead to cramming the night before, which will cause you to be physically and mentally exhausted for the test. Poor time management also contributes to feelings of stress, fear, and hopelessness as you realize you are not well prepared but don't know what to do about it.

Other times, test anxiety is not related to your preparation for the test but comes from unresolved fear. This may be a past failure on a test, or poor performance on tests in general. It may come from comparing yourself to others who seem to be performing better or from the stress of living up to expectations. Anxiety may be driven by fears of the future—how failure on this test would affect your educational and career goals. These fears are often completely irrational, but they can still negatively impact your test performance.

Review Video: <u>3 Reasons You Have Test Anxiety</u>
Visit mometrix.com/academy and enter code: 428468

150

Elements of Test Anxiety

As mentioned earlier, test anxiety is considered to be an emotional state, but it has physical and mental components as well. Sometimes you may not even realize that you are suffering from test anxiety until you notice the physical symptoms. These can include trembling hands, rapid heartbeat, sweating, nausea, and tense muscles. Extreme anxiety may lead to fainting or vomiting. Obviously, any of these symptoms can have a negative impact on testing. It is important to recognize them as soon as they begin to occur so that you can address the problem before it damages your performance.

Review Video: 3 Ways to Tell You Have Test Anxiety
Visit mometrix.com/academy and enter code: 927847

The mental components of test anxiety include trouble focusing and inability to remember learned information. During a test, your mind is on high alert, which can help you recall information and stay focused for an extended period of time. However, anxiety interferes with your mind's natural processes, causing you to blank out, even on the questions you know well. The strain of testing during anxiety makes it difficult to stay focused, especially on a test that may take several hours. Extreme anxiety can take a huge mental toll, making it difficult not only to recall test information but even to understand the test questions or pull your thoughts together.

Review Video: How Test Anxiety Affects Memory
Visit mometrix.com/academy and enter code: 609003

Effects of Test Anxiety

Test anxiety is like a disease—if left untreated, it will get progressively worse. Anxiety leads to poor performance, and this reinforces the feelings of fear and failure, which in turn lead to poor performances on subsequent tests. It can grow from a mild nervousness to a crippling condition. If allowed to progress, test anxiety can have a big impact on your schooling, and consequently on your future.

Test anxiety can spread to other parts of your life. Anxiety on tests can become anxiety in any stressful situation, and blanking on a test can turn into panicking in a job situation. But fortunately, you don't have to let anxiety rule your testing and determine your grades. There are a number of relatively simple steps you can take to move past anxiety and function normally on a test and in the rest of life.

Review Video: How Test Anxiety Impacts Your Grades
Visit mometrix.com/academy and enter code: 939819

Physical Steps for Beating Test Anxiety

While test anxiety is a serious problem, the good news is that it can be overcome. It doesn't have to control your ability to think and remember information. While it may take time, you can begin taking steps today to beat anxiety.

Just as your first hint that you may be struggling with anxiety comes from the physical symptoms, the first step to treating it is also physical. Rest is crucial for having a clear, strong mind. If you are tired, it is much easier to give in to anxiety. But if you establish good sleep habits, your body and mind will be ready to perform optimally, without the strain of exhaustion. Additionally, sleeping well helps you to retain information better, so you're more likely to recall the answers when you see the test questions.

Getting good sleep means more than going to bed on time. It's important to allow your brain time to relax. Take study breaks from time to time so it doesn't get overworked, and don't study right before bed. Take time to rest your mind before trying to rest your body, or you may find it difficult to fall asleep.

Review Video: <u>The Importance of Sleep for Your Brain</u>
Visit mometrix.com/academy and enter code: 319338

Along with sleep, other aspects of physical health are important in preparing for a test. Good nutrition is vital for good brain function. Sugary foods and drinks may give a burst of energy but this burst is followed by a crash, both physically and emotionally. Instead, fuel your body with protein and vitamin-rich foods.

Also, drink plenty of water. Dehydration can lead to headaches and exhaustion, especially if your brain is already under stress from the rigors of the test. Particularly if your test is a long one, drink water during the breaks. And if possible, take an energy-boosting snack to eat between sections.

Review Video: <u>How Diet Can Affect your Mood</u>
Visit mometrix.com/academy and enter code: 624317

Along with sleep and diet, a third important part of physical health is exercise. Maintaining a steady workout schedule is helpful, but even taking 5-minute study breaks to walk can help get your blood pumping faster and clear your head. Exercise also releases endorphins, which contribute to a positive feeling and can help combat test anxiety.

When you nurture your physical health, you are also contributing to your mental health. If your body is healthy, your mind is much more likely to be healthy as well. So take time to rest, nourish your body with healthy food and water, and get moving as much as possible. Taking these physical steps will make you stronger and more able to take the mental steps necessary to overcome test anxiety.

Review Video: <u>How to Stay Healthy and Prevent Test Anxiety</u>
Visit mometrix.com/academy and enter code: 877894

Mental Steps for Beating Test Anxiety

Working on the mental side of test anxiety can be more challenging, but as with the physical side, there are clear steps you can take to overcome it. As mentioned earlier, test anxiety often stems from lack of preparation, so the obvious solution is to prepare for the test. Effective studying may be the most important weapon you have for beating test anxiety, but you can and should employ several other mental tools to combat fear.

First, boost your confidence by reminding yourself of past success—tests or projects that you aced. If you're putting as much effort into preparing for this test as you did for those, there's no reason you should expect to fail here. Work hard to prepare; then trust your preparation.

Second, surround yourself with encouraging people. It can be helpful to find a study group, but be sure that the people you're around will encourage a positive attitude. If you spend time with others who are anxious or cynical, this will only contribute to your own anxiety. Look for others who are motivated to study hard from a desire to succeed, not from a fear of failure.

Third, reward yourself. A test is physically and mentally tiring, even without anxiety, and it can be helpful to have something to look forward to. Plan an activity following the test, regardless of the outcome, such as going to a movie or getting ice cream.

When you are taking the test, if you find yourself beginning to feel anxious, remind yourself that you know the material. Visualize successfully completing the test. Then take a few deep, relaxing breaths and return to it. Work through the questions carefully but with confidence, knowing that you are capable of succeeding.

Developing a healthy mental approach to test taking will also aid in other areas of life. Test anxiety affects more than just the actual test—it can be damaging to your mental health and even contribute to depression. It's important to beat test anxiety before it becomes a problem for more than testing.

Review Video: Test Anxiety and Depression
Visit mometrix.com/academy and enter code: 904704

Study Strategy

Being prepared for the test is necessary to combat anxiety, but what does being prepared look like? You may study for hours on end and still not feel prepared. What you need is a strategy for test prep. The next few pages outline our recommended steps to help you plan out and conquer the challenge of preparation.

STEP 1: SCOPE OUT THE TEST

Learn everything you can about the format (multiple choice, essay, etc.) and what will be on the test. Gather any study materials, course outlines, or sample exams that may be available. Not only will this help you to prepare, but knowing what to expect can help to alleviate test anxiety.

STEP 2: MAP OUT THE MATERIAL

Look through the textbook or study guide and make note of how many chapters or sections it has. Then divide these over the time you have. For example, if a book has 15 chapters and you have five days to study, you need to cover three chapters each day. Even better, if you have the time, leave an extra day at the end for overall review after you have gone through the material in depth.

If time is limited, you may need to prioritize the material. Look through it and make note of which sections you think you already have a good grasp on, and which need review. While you are studying, skim quickly through the familiar sections and take more time on the challenging parts. Write out your plan so you don't get lost as you go. Having a written plan also helps you feel more in control of the study, so anxiety is less likely to arise from feeling overwhelmed at the amount to cover.

STEP 3: GATHER YOUR TOOLS

Decide what study method works best for you. Do you prefer to highlight in the book as you study and then go back over the highlighted portions? Or do you type out notes of the important information? Or is it helpful to make flashcards that you can carry with you? Assemble the pens, index cards, highlighters, post-it notes, and any other materials you may need so you won't be distracted by getting up to find things while you study.

If you're having a hard time retaining the information or organizing your notes, experiment with different methods. For example, try color-coding by subject with colored pens, highlighters, or post-it notes. If you learn better by hearing, try recording yourself reading your notes so you can listen while in the car, working out, or simply sitting at your desk. Ask a friend to quiz you from your flashcards, or try teaching someone the material to solidify it in your mind.

STEP 4: CREATE YOUR ENVIRONMENT

It's important to avoid distractions while you study. This includes both the obvious distractions like visitors and the subtle distractions like an uncomfortable chair (or a too-comfortable couch that makes you want to fall asleep). Set up the best study environment possible: good lighting and a comfortable work area. If background music helps you focus, you may want to turn it on, but otherwise keep the room quiet. If you are using a computer to take notes, be sure you don't have any other windows open, especially applications like social media, games, or anything else that could distract you. Silence your phone and turn off notifications. Be sure to keep water close by so you stay hydrated while you study (but avoid unhealthy drinks and snacks).

Also, take into account the best time of day to study. Are you freshest first thing in the morning? Try to set aside some time then to work through the material. Is your mind clearer in the afternoon or evening? Schedule your study session then. Another method is to study at the same time of day that you will take the test, so that your brain gets used to working on the material at that time and will be ready to focus at test time.

STEP 5: STUDY!

Once you have done all the study preparation, it's time to settle into the actual studying. Sit down, take a few moments to settle your mind so you can focus, and begin to follow your study plan. Don't give in to distractions or let yourself procrastinate. This is your time to prepare so you'll be ready to fearlessly approach the test. Make the most of the time and stay focused.

Of course, you don't want to burn out. If you study too long you may find that you're not retaining the information very well. Take regular study breaks. For example, taking five minutes out of every hour to walk briskly, breathing deeply and swinging your arms, can help your mind stay fresh.

As you get to the end of each chapter or section, it's a good idea to do a quick review. Remind yourself of what you learned and work on any difficult parts. When you feel that you've mastered the material, move on to the next part. At the end of your study session, briefly skim through your notes again.

But while review is helpful, cramming last minute is NOT. If at all possible, work ahead so that you won't need to fit all your study into the last day. Cramming overloads your brain with more information than it can process and retain, and your tired mind may struggle to recall even previously learned information when it is overwhelmed with last-minute study. Also, the urgent nature of cramming and the stress placed on your brain contribute to anxiety. You'll be more likely to go to the test feeling unprepared and having trouble thinking clearly.

So don't cram, and don't stay up late before the test, even just to review your notes at a leisurely pace. Your brain needs rest more than it needs to go over the information again. In fact, plan to finish your studies by noon or early afternoon the day before the test. Give your brain the rest of the day to relax or focus on other things, and get a good night's sleep. Then you will be fresh for the test and better able to recall what you've studied.

STEP 6: TAKE A PRACTICE TEST

Many courses offer sample tests, either online or in the study materials. This is an excellent resource to check whether you have mastered the material, as well as to prepare for the test format and environment.

Check the test format ahead of time: the number of questions, the type (multiple choice, free response, etc.), and the time limit. Then create a plan for working through them. For example, if you have 30 minutes to take a 60-question test, your limit is 30 seconds per question. Spend less time on the questions you know well so that you can take more time on the difficult ones.

If you have time to take several practice tests, take the first one open book, with no time limit. Work through the questions at your own pace and make sure you fully understand them. Gradually work up to taking a test under test conditions: sit at a desk with all study materials put away and set a timer. Pace yourself to make sure you finish the test with time to spare and go back to check your answers if you have time.

After each test, check your answers. On the questions you missed, be sure you understand why you missed them. Did you misread the question (tests can use tricky wording)? Did you forget the information? Or was it something you hadn't learned? Go back and study any shaky areas that the practice tests reveal.

Taking these tests not only helps with your grade, but also aids in combating test anxiety. If you're already used to the test conditions, you're less likely to worry about it, and working through tests until you're scoring well gives you a confidence boost. Go through the practice tests until you feel comfortable, and then you can go into the test knowing that you're ready for it.

Test Tips

On test day, you should be confident, knowing that you've prepared well and are ready to answer the questions. But aside from preparation, there are several test day strategies you can employ to maximize your performance.

First, as stated before, get a good night's sleep the night before the test (and for several nights before that, if possible). Go into the test with a fresh, alert mind rather than staying up late to study.

Try not to change too much about your normal routine on the day of the test. It's important to eat a nutritious breakfast, but if you normally don't eat breakfast at all, consider eating just a protein bar. If you're a coffee drinker, go ahead and have your normal coffee. Just make sure you time it so that the caffeine doesn't wear off right in the middle of your test. Avoid sugary beverages, and drink enough water to stay hydrated but not so much that you need a restroom break 10 minutes into the test. If your test isn't first thing in the morning, consider going for a walk or doing a light workout before the test to get your blood flowing.

Allow yourself enough time to get ready, and leave for the test with plenty of time to spare so you won't have the anxiety of scrambling to arrive in time. Another reason to be early is to select a good seat. It's helpful to sit away from doors and windows, which can be distracting. Find a good seat, get out your supplies, and settle your mind before the test begins.

When the test begins, start by going over the instructions carefully, even if you already know what to expect. Make sure you avoid any careless mistakes by following the directions.

Then begin working through the questions, pacing yourself as you've practiced. If you're not sure on an answer, don't spend too much time on it, and don't let it shake your confidence. Either skip it and come back later, or eliminate as many wrong answers as possible and guess among the remaining ones. Don't dwell on these questions as you continue—put them out of your mind and focus on what lies ahead.

Be sure to read all of the answer choices, even if you're sure the first one is the right answer. Sometimes you'll find a better one if you keep reading. But don't second-guess yourself if you do immediately know the answer. Your gut instinct is usually right. Don't let test anxiety rob you of the information you know.

If you have time at the end of the test (and if the test format allows), go back and review your answers. Be cautious about changing any, since your first instinct tends to be correct, but make sure you didn't misread any of the questions or accidentally mark the wrong answer choice. Look over any you skipped and make an educated guess.

At the end, leave the test feeling confident. You've done your best, so don't waste time worrying about your performance or wishing you could change anything. Instead, celebrate the successful

completion of this test. And finally, use this test to learn how to deal with anxiety even better next time.

Important Qualification

Not all anxiety is created equal. If your test anxiety is causing major issues in your life beyond the classroom or testing center, or if you are experiencing troubling physical symptoms related to your anxiety, it may be a sign of a serious physiological or psychological condition. If this sounds like your situation, we strongly encourage you to seek professional help.

Thank You

We at Mometrix would like to extend our heartfelt thanks to you, our friend and patron, for allowing us to play a part in your journey. It is a privilege to serve people from all walks of life who are unified in their commitment to building the best future they can for themselves.

The preparation you devote to these important testing milestones may be the most valuable educational opportunity you have for making a real difference in your life. We encourage you to put your heart into it—that feeling of succeeding, overcoming, and yes, conquering will be well worth the hours you've invested.

We want to hear your story, your struggles and your successes, and if you see any opportunities for us to improve our materials so we can help others even more effectively in the future, please share that with us as well. **The team at Mometrix would be absolutely thrilled to hear from you!** So please, send us an email (support@mometrix.com) and let's stay in touch.

If you'd like some additional help, check out these other resources we offer for your exam:
http://MometrixFlashcards.com/PropertyCasualty

Additional Bonus Material

Due to our efforts to try to keep this book to a manageable length, we've created a link that will give you access to all of your additional bonus material.

Please visit
https://www.mometrix.com/bonus948/propertycasual to
access the information.